PLAYING GROWN-UP IS SERIOUS BUSINESS

PLAYING GROWN-UP IS SERIOUS BUSINESS

BREAKING FREE

OF ADDICTIVE

FAMILY PATTERNS

DR BARRY WEINHOLD

STILLPOINT

STILLPOINT PUBLISHING
Products and technologies for creating the EXTRAordinary life
For a free catalog or ordering information
write:
Stillpoint Publishing, Box 640, Walpole, NH 03608 USA
or call:
1-800-847-4014 TOLL-FREE
(Continental US, except NH)
1-603-756-9281
(Foreign and NH)

This book is manufactured in the United States of America.
Text and cover design by Rostislav Eismont, Richmond, NH
Published by Stillpoint Publishing, a division of
Stillpoint International, Inc.
Box 640, Meetinghouse Road, Walpole, NH 03608.

Published simultaneously in Canada by
Fitzhenry & Whiteside Ltd., Toronto

Library of Congress Card Catalog Number 88-06-870
Weinhold, Barry K.
Playing Grown-up is Serious Business
ISBN 0-913299-51-0 First Trade Paper Edition
9 8 7 6 5 4 3 2

This book is printed on acid-free 100% recycled paper to
save trees and preserve Earth's ecology.

DEDICATION

This book is dedicated to the
memory of Barbara MacDougald Weinhold
(1932-1983)

Contents

CONTENTS

CONTENTS

CONTENTS

CONTENTS

Acknowledgments

This book would not have been possible without the help of countless professionals, students and clients who participated in my *Breaking Family Patterns* workshops and seminars and in individual and group therapy with me. Special thanks to Dr. Arnold Mindell of Zurich, Switzerland who read parts of the manuscript. In addition, I would like to acknowledge Barbara MacDougald Weinhold who helped me conduct *Breaking Family Patterns* workshops and seminars until her death in 1983. Since 1986, Janae Weinhold has been co-leading therapy groups with me. In addition, she typed the original manuscript and provided me with editing and typing assistance on the final manuscript.

All the proceeds from the sale of this book are being donated to the Colorado Institute for Conflict Resolution and Creative Leadership. This Institute is a non-profit, tax-exempt organization that was formed to actively promote the cause of world peace. Everyone who breaks his or her dysfunctional patterns is, in effect, also making this world a little bit better place to live in and is therefore supporting the cause of world peace.

PART I

THE LOSS OF
THE TRUE SELF

Introduction

This book examines the basic psychological causes of all human misery. It is written to make adults more aware of the attitudes and behavior patterns that they learned during childhood. These dysfunctional, addictive family patterns are often forgotten until adulthood when they begin to interfere with relationships. It is my contention that these unconscious patterns are responsible for most of the cruelty that human beings administer to themselves and others. Behind all emotional, sexual and physical child abuse; behind all crimes of violence; behind all eating disorders, alcoholism and drug abuse; behind teenage suicides; behind all unhappy and co-dependent relationships and perhaps behind all illnesses lurk dysfunctional ways of thinking, feeling and behaving that we learned as children from our family of origin.

It takes considerable spiritual courage and persistence to examine your life and begin to become aware of the similarities between your present behavior and the past hurts or woundings you suffered as a child. The problem of recovery of the past is made more difficult because 1) many times the damage was done so early in life (before you were two years old) that now you are unable to remember any of the actual events or their effects on you, and 2) you believed and ac-

1

tually may have been told that what was done to you by your parents was done *for your own good.*

In addition to the overt physical and sexual abuse of children, there is a great deal of psychological abuse done to children. Children are ridiculed, teased, taunted, not taken seriously, not respected as people with rights, made instruments to satisfy the needs of others, not listened to and deprived of the tools necessary to become fully functioning, independent adults. *As long as you are unable to see the harmful effects of what was done to you during your childhood, you will have an unconscious compulsion to inflict these hurts on others when you become an adult.* You may continue to "beat yourself up" with internalized self-condemnation, or you may find a weaker, more helpless victim on whom you can take out your revenge for what was done to you. Quite often that weaker, more helpless victim is one of your own children or your spouse or employees placed under your supervision. You may be driven to even the score by "identifying with the aggressor" and doing unto others what was done to you.

The first half of the book describes the general and specific addictive patterns of feelings and behaviors that you learned from your family of origin and unwittingly carry over into your adult relationships. These patterns represent unresolved issues and unhealed wounds that press for resolution and healing in your current relationships. Without awareness of the source of these patterns, you can literally destroy or damage severely your current relationships. The book provides awareness activities to help you personalize the patterns and begin to examine effects of the behavior patterns on your current relationships.

The second half of the book deals with the process of breaking these dysfunctional, addictive family patterns and the process of replacing them with healthier and more functional behaviors. We now know a lot about the process of how people get broken, and we also now know the process they need to use to fix what got broken. Case material drawn from my practice as a psychologist, as well as examples from my own personal struggle to become aware of these patterns, are presented.

The purpose of the book is not to attribute blame to your parents but rather to help you see what happened and why. Part of this process involves being able to see that your parents were also victims of this curse and were unable to fix their broken parts before they became parents. Compulsively, without full awareness, they passed on the effects of their pain and suffering to the next generation.

Your full awareness of this process can eventually lead you to feel compassion toward your parents and truly forgive their acts. However, before you can do that you must examine what really happened to you and what harmful effects these events had on you. You must be able to feel the pain, experience the unhealed wounds and express the anger and the hatred, before you can move to deeper feelings of sadness and compassion. To do this essential emotional work, many people seek the assistance of a trained therapist, while others are able to get the support they need for this work from friends and loved ones. In either case, you need a sense of protection to enable you to dig deep into your psyche and uncover these unexpressed feelings.

As a psychologist, I see people suffering real pain and confusion as a result of these unconscious, addictive behavior patterns that are ruining their lives and their relationships. Mostly they are reenacting scenes from their childhood, still trying in rather unskilled ways to understand what really happened and then becoming even more angry and frustrated at the unwillingness of their partner to let them play out the scenes the way they would like so they can understand how and why things went wrong. We all have an unconscious drive toward wholeness and healing, but what we lack are the tools and understandings to make that possible.

Many professional psychiatrists, psychologists and other psychotherapists have long contended that these patterns learned in childhood can only be changed through the use of long-term psychotherapy, and even then the success rate is limited. My strong belief is that the tools for changing these patterns, once the dominion of only a few trained professionals, now have to be made available to everyone. We know that many people will never be able to afford long-term psychotherapy and, even if they could afford it, they probably would not go. With the use of the information, tools and skills presented in this book, many people can and will change their lives in positive ways. The book can be considered by support groups such as Alcoholics Anonymous, Al-Anon, Adult Children of Alcoholics and Adult Children of Dysfunctional Families to help people do this deeper healing work.

I believe that parents do not need extensive training to stop the

3

vicious cycle of cruelty they often inflict on their children. What they do need is to consciously refrain from trying to control their children to satisfy their own needs and to stop trying to suppress any expression of feelings by their children. Instead, if parents can endeavor to understand their children, show respect for their needs, listen to their feelings and take them seriously, parents will go a long way toward providing a solid foundation from which their children can grow up and develop their own lives.

We have a long way to go because, according to various estimates, as many as 97 out of 100 families may be dysfunctional and addictive in some major areas. The other three families probably are in a recovery stage.

Many people grow up being unaware of the dysfunctional and addictive nature of their family of origin. The following is a list of characteristics of a dysfunctional family.

1. Rigid and compulsive rules. Lots of rules that everyone has to follow perfectly or they get into trouble.

2. Rigid and compulsive roles. There are prescribed roles given to everyone, usually with little choice: "He is the smart one and she is the pretty one."

3. Family secrets. Lots of things that happen are kept secret from others in the family.

4. Very serious and burdened. Very little humor unless it is making fun of people or having children be the butt of jokes.

5. No personal privacy and unclear personal boundaries. Children often *have* to share their personal space, their clothing and their toys to the extent that they have no personal belongings.

6. False sense of loyalty to the family. This is used to control children and keep them dependent on the family.

7. Resistance to outsiders. There is a "we versus them" attitude.

8. Strong feelings are not permitted. Compulsive and addictive behaviors are utilized to suppress or avoid any strong feelings.

9. Conflict between family members is denied and ignored.

10. The family resists change. They are afraid to try new things.

11. There is no unity. The family is very fragmented. There is a feeling of isolation and a lack of protection. Family members triangulate to get support by creating alliances with other family members.

4

There is no such thing as a totally dysfunctional family, but if you see your birth family as having a number of these characteristics, then it is likely your family was dysfunctional in some important ways.

When large numbers of people are able to understand their plight and begin to take steps to heal their childhood wounds, instead of wounding others, only then will our society change. Only then will we insist that parents be given these simple tools and understandings necessary for them to raise effective children. Only then will the curriculum of our schools truly reflect the social, emotional, psychological as well as intellectual needs of our children. Only then will our national priorities reflect the importance of raising free children to live in a free society. It has been said that the best way to judge a culture is by examining the way it treats its children. At present we would not get very high marks by this criterion. This book examines why we have treated our children so poorly and provides straightforward ideas on how we can change that condition as well as providing practical suggestions on how we can heal our own wounds from childhood.

Finally, this book represents an emerging paradigm in the helping professions. The old paradigm is diagnostic and remedial, where people are treated as sick, given a diagnosis and then given some treatment or drug to make them well. This paradigm also tends to identify psychological states (depression, anxiety, hypomanic states, etc.) but *not* the psychological processes through which people can change states.

This new, emerging paradigm is process-oriented and preventative. The emphasis in the new paradigm is on giving people the tools necessary to help them move through psychological states and not get stuck in any one state, like depression. Instead of treating problems strictly as symptoms of a psychological illness, problems are seen as a normal part of the natural human process of moving to more complete and whole states of being. Thus symptoms are viewed as *right* or having some important function as part of a healing process trying to happen. This helps empower people and gives them a better chance of meeting life's challenges with confidence and courage.

CHAPTER ONE

The Sins of the Father

Our lives are simply
Threads pulling along
The lasting thoughts
Which travel through
Time that way

—NANCY WOOD
MANY WINTERS

He was the son of a middle-class government worker. His father demanded absolute obedience from his children and was given to fits of rage with his family. This boy, when he was three, witnessed his father brutally beating his mother for talking back to her husband. When the boy was four, his father began to physically beat him on a daily basis. At six he remembered getting thirty lashes on his back with a whip. When his father wanted him, he would whistle for him as one would call a dog. At age eleven he was almost beaten to death by his father when he attempted to run away.

Before this boy was born, three of his siblings had died of diphtheria, all before they were three years old and all within one month of another. His mother, fearful of losing another child, kept her distance from this boy and never fully bonded with him. His father, often drunk, launched into long diatribes about how the Jews and other minorities were causing all the world's problems. The boy grew to hate his father, but he found no safe outlets for his feelings. He began to bully other boys, play violent war games and give speeches of hatred toward Jews and other minorities.

This boy grew into a hateful man who never married or had a family of his own on whom he could act out his feelings, and instead he found a larger context for the expression of his hatred. He subjected a whole race to his hatred—this boy grew up to be Adolph Hitler. (Miller 1983)

Any report of overt violence in the family seems to somehow shock our sensibilities, which are usually quieted by some reassuring internal message like, "What can you expect from those (add your favorite racial or socioeconomic slur)," or we may say to ourselves, "If only they had gone to church this wouldn't have happened" or "That's what happens in those broken homes." Then we go on our smug way, never questioning our stereotypes and definitely not looking at our own potential for violent behavior. Some observers have said we live in the most violent country on earth, and the overtness of that violence seems to be increasing rapidly. Strangely, the targets for that violence are often family members and children.

Recognizing that, you may be more interested than most in discovering the real causes of violence in the family and understanding why certain patterns of destructive behavior do tend to repeat themselves in each family generation. I will present a brief overview of how I see the problem and then move into more specific causes. Summary statistics are used here to highlight the breadth of the problem, help set the stage and provide some background to orient you to what is to come.

The Family War Zone

According to Dr. Joyce Brothers (1984), "Each year, almost 1.8 million women are regularly beaten in their homes by men who once promised to love and cherish them for life." Another nationwide study (Strau et al. 1980) showed that if you are married, the chances you will be slugged by your spouse are between one in four and one in three. The same study indicated that between 3.4 million and 4 million children have been "beaten up" by a parent. Finally, their study showed that as many as 1.8 million children between the ages of three and seventeen have been threatened with a knife or gun by a parent.

When you add sexual abuse into these figures, you get an even greater awareness of the extent of the problem. Author Susan Forward says, "There are probably more than ten million Americans who have been involved in incest, and they come from every economic, cultural, racial, educational, religious and geographical background." (Forward and Buck 1978)

Various studies on the incidence of sexual child abuse estimate

7

that up to one in every four women in the United States is a victim of sexual molestation by the time she reaches the age of eighteen. (Walker 1979) In addition to the immediate psychological and emotional effects of sexual abuse, many long-term problems can result. This kind of violation can have long-term effects on a person's self-esteem, with lingering guilt and shame that lead to repression and denial of feelings, or they may lead to compulsive behaviors such as eating disorders, suicide, crime and other social problems. For example, many women who experienced a terrorizing sexual experience as a child have trouble enjoying sex as adults, often with no understanding of the causes of their dysfunction. Frequently, victims of sexual abuse are in their thirties or forties before they actually remember the incidents and their feelings of terror from their childhood. (Forward 1978)

What makes this problem even more acute is the fact that most of these destructive patterns are passed directly on to the next generation, and the cycle of abuse goes on unbroken. Most people are shocked when they hear of someone who was abused physically or sexually as a child now being identified as an abuser of his/her own children. We may try to dismiss this by saying to ourselves that this only happens to a small number of people. However, if you are honest, you probably remember after being "victimized" or treated poorly by your parents when you were a child that you vowed never to treat your children that way, only to find yourself in times of stress repeating almost the same words and behaviors of your parents on your own children.

Despite your best intentions, there seems to be built into you a "compulsion to repeat" these acts of cruelty. This may help you to understand why abuse patterns of behavior are often repeated generation after generation. This compulsion to repeat acts of cruelty is also called the *talionic impulse* (Masterson 1981) and may be one of the deepest and most ancient of human impulses—to get revenge by inflicting on others weaker than you the hurt you experienced when you were in a weak and vulnerable position. The Old Testament speaks of "an eye for an eye and a tooth for a tooth." Actually, the development of an objective sense of what is right and wrong about human behavior is a relatively new social concept in the evolution of society, and it came as the result of a long and slow social process over thousands of years.

8

This covert impulse was woven right into the social and legal fabric. In the Middle Ages, writes Nietzsche (1955), "to behold suffering gave pleasure, but to cause another to suffer afforded an even greater pleasure . . . a royal wedding or great public celebration would have been incomplete without executions, tortures or auto-da-fé . . . there was scarcely a noble household without some person whose office it was to serve as a butt for everyone's malice and cruel teasing." Legally, people "could cut out an amount of flesh proportionate to the amount of the debt, and we find, very early, quite detailed assessments of the value of individual parts of the body."

As these socially sanctioned expressions of the talionic impulse disappeared, the compulsion was internalized and made part of child-rearing practices. Alice Miller (1983) writes the following: "When we examine the child-rearing literature of the past two-hundred years, we discover the methods that have systematically been used to make it impossible for children to realize and later to remember the way they were actually treated by their parents."

One famous book on child-rearing written in 1899 states ". . . if parents are fortunate to drive out willfulness from the very beginning by means of scolding and the rod, they will have obedient, docile, and good children . . ." (Schotzman 1973)

In the eighteenth and nineteenth centuries these attitudes of oppression and control were still stated openly, but in modern books on child-rearing practices the authors attempt to conceal and are careful to justify any attempts to dominate a child. Take the following example from a book written in 1975 by a pair of psychologists: Three boys aged eight, eleven and fourteen were assigned household tasks and assigned times in which to do them. If they did not do their tasks to the satisfaction of their parents, ". . . no plate on the dinner table; boy, calmly denied privilege of supper. . . . Parents were able to let the situation do the punishing and become 'benevolent disapprovers.'" The authors (Madsen & Madsen 1975) don't mention that the parents were the ones who set up the situation. They admitted that "Later the mother confessed that when he (her son) was hungry she really wanted to fix a snack for him, late at night." As you can see, the talionic impulse has found a new home in our child-rearing practices, fully supported by psychologists, psychiatrists and educators. Let me trace briefly how this process seems to operate in families.

9

The Vicious Cycle of Cruelty

We can begin to see this process more clearly in a "normal" context when we begin to understand that because of the way we raise children, there isn't any one of us who reaches adulthood without experiencing serious "wounds" to our psyche. These would include all the times you were not taken seriously, made fun of, not allowed to express what you really felt, not respected as a person with a will of your own, and an endless variety of hurts you suffered when you were told to "get lost", "shut up", "get out of here", "don't act so -----" or "don't be so -----." All of these left their marks on you in the form of wounds to your self-esteem.

Because you likely perceived that it was not safe to express your true feelings toward those doing the wounding, what you most likely did with those wounds was try to get even by expressing your anger toward someone you perceived as weaker than you. The other alternative was to devalue yourself as apparently unworthy and deserving of punishment. This latter option may have been supported by your parents, who told you that what was being done to you was being done by intelligent, all-knowing parents who were doing it to you for your own good. (Miller 1983) You really had no one who understood how you felt nor anyone who could help you understand and validate your feelings. You truly must have felt like a stranger in a strange land. As a result, you may have repressed these feelings and the wounds remained unhealed into adulthood. You may have tried your best to work it out with your parents while you were growing up, but you lacked the understanding of what the problem was and you lacked the tools necessary to solve the problem.

There is an old adage that says, "You can't fix something until you know how it was broken." Without an understanding of what really happened to you and why your parents treated you the way they did, there is little hope of fixing the brokenness you may feel. As an adult you have to work it out the best way you can. It is not surprising that many times you may unconsciously seek a relationship with someone who you hope will finally understand and help you heal these wounds. But again, because the process is not a conscious one and because you cannot control your partner the way you would like to, you again end up not getting the understanding you seek and end up feeling even more wounded.

If all attempts seem to fail to bring you the desired results, you may give up and try to work it out with your own children, or with others who you perceive to be weaker or less able than you and who you *think* you can control. Now you can do to them what was done to you—but without guilt because you truly believe you are doing it to them for their own good. It seems that as long as you do not recognize or understand the harmful effects of what was done to you as a child, you are destined to repeat those acts of cruelty, without seeing them as cruel acts. Instead, you may even defend or justify your behavior, as did your parents, as being necessary to raise your children to know some of the following seemingly important social values:

1. having respect for their elders at all times
2. having a low opinion of themselves, appearing modest
3. seeing their parents as always right
4. never expressing any strong feelings
5. acting nice (even when they don't feel nice)
6. pretending to be grateful even when they don't feel that way
7. being strong, tough and able to take a joke, punishment, etc.
8. being obedient
9. feeling duty-bound to love their parents
10. not being strong-willed or obstinate

The methods most parents use to "teach" these qualities provide even clearer indications of what was really going on. Feeling completely justified, parents will: lay traps, lie and use duplicity, subterfuge and manipulation; make threats of violence; do actual violence; withdraw their love; use isolation, distrust, humiliation, scorn, ridicule, coercion and, if necessary, physical or mental torture. Frequently, these methods are employed unwittingly through a lack of understanding of the real needs of children.

Recently, while sitting in an airport waiting for a flight, I witnessed a situation similar to one described in Alice Miller's *The Drama of the Gifted Child* (1981). Two well-dressed parents with a child about two years old were also waiting for an airplane. While waiting, they each got a candy bar out of a machine and the mother began to share some of her candy with the child. The child began to whine and cry and kept saying, "Mine, too." The mother would respond by giving him another bite of her candy bar, only to have him shake his head vigorously and repeat his plea for a candy bar of his own. The parents, who were obviously preoccupied by some other matter, kept talking to each other and ignored the child's repeated pleas. He started throwing himself on the floor and began kicking the floor and crying even louder. At this, the mother grabbed the child and began hitting him on the rear and quickly carried him off down the concourse, threatening him with more physical punishment if he didn't stop crying. The father, during this outburst, looked helplessly at me, shrugged his shoulders and sat down to read his newspaper.

It seemed rather clear to me that this boy was not trying to act in any disrespectful way toward his parents but was operating out of a strong need to have a candy bar of his own so he could be equal to his parents who each had one. This is a normal need for a two-year-old who is trying to imitate adult behavior in order to learn how to become a fully functioning individual. Had the parents understood his need, one of them could have given him his/her candy bar and then asked the little boy to give one of them a bite from "his" candy bar. It is likely if he had satisfied his need to have a candy bar of his own, he would have gladly shared it with one or both of his parents.

When our needs are satisfied, we are free to act in ways that enable others, in turn, to satisfy their own needs. I wondered what frustrations these parents must have endured as children, and I noted how their lack of understanding of their own parents' behavior must have blinded them in this situation from seeing an obvious solution to the problem. It is certain that both parents and the little boy felt bad about what was happening, and everyone missed an opportunity to increase his/her sense of well-being. One might ask: Why didn't these parents have some empathy for this child because of the memory of their own unhealed emotional wounds from being treated the same way as a child? Part of the answer to this riddle comes from seeing these parents as insecure children themselves in that situation, perhaps being flooded by internal cues and feelings that prevented them from making new responses to their child. They were likely "fused" into old response patterns from which they could either do nothing and feel bad, as they probably did as a child, or they could respond the only other way they knew, which likely was the way their parents behaved toward them.

Actually, there is another reason why they could have behaved the way they did. The reason is that their response or lack of appropriate response helped them to avoid their own unpleasant feelings of helplessness and emotional abandonment from childhood that likely were triggered by this situation. Because they are still unaware of the connection with their own childhood and are cut off from their true feelings, they do not understand how to handle situations like this one any differently. In this way, the cruelty and contempt you display toward those who are smaller and weaker helps you deny your own feelings of helplessness. If you were not afraid of these feelings, you could allow yourself to feel the feelings and begin to understand where they are coming from instead of "puffing up" and acting angry toward a weaker person. Interestingly, you may not even know you have these feelings of helplessness, jealousy and loneliness lurking inside of you until something appears to trigger a strong emotional response.

Part of the reason for this denial is that you may have experienced these feelings so early in life that you truly don't remember the feelings or the incidents causing the feelings. In your innocence, you could not understand why you were not allowed to express your true nature, and, to make matters worse, you were often told that what was being done to you was being done *for your own good*. When you become a parent, it seems almost necessary to do the same things to your own children to prove to yourself that your parents really did love you. This makes the denial even harder to reach and change. You also may have tried to avoid your feelings as a child, knowing you would be punished even more for expressing your feelings, and now as an adult you continue to use ways of avoiding these feelings.

As an adult you may be afraid of these unintegrated feelings that seem to pop up unexpectedly and you may fear that you will be overwhelmed by the feelings. You may do almost anything to avoid feeling them and to maintain your denial. This denial and repression of feelings of anger, hurt, sadness and fear from your childhood are what trap you most. Unless these feelings are identified correctly and expressed fully, it is not possible to break out of the vicious cycle of cruelty. You will compulsively and unwittingly pass on this cruelty to your children, who then are likely to do the same with their children.

The only effective ways to break the cycle are to: 1) reexamine your childhood experiences, 2) change your perceptions of what really happened to you and 3) fully express any and all feelings that were not expressed as a child. The full expression can be done safely without doing harm to yourself or your parents or anyone else, for that matter. You must be able to see and admit that you truly are an adult child of a dysfunctional family before you can correct your perceptions. This book will provide you with information to help you unravel the events of your childhood and help you correct your perceptions about what happened to you. In addition, this book will provide you with many suggestions and exercises for releasing childhood feelings.

Had you been able to express these feelings as a child and had you been given empathetic responses from a parent or other adult, there would be no need for you to defend against these feelings as an adult. This in itself frees you to respond more empathetically to your children when they express normal childhood needs and feelings. We know that parents who had their childhood needs attended to by understanding, supportive parents are free to do that for their children, instead of being trapped in compulsive, reactive and destructive response patterns. Since you likely didn't get this support as a child, you may find yourself as a parent engaging in unskilled behavior, and you may find yourself involved in a mutual on-the-job-training project to grow up.

Children As Our Teachers

In the candy bar example, if these parents had understood what was being triggered in them and had learned a few effective communication skills, they could have used similar situations to both heal their own wounds and to avoid creating new wounds in their offspring. It has been said that our children are our best teachers because they will bring up in us everything that was left unresolved in us from our childhood. They will present you with situations where you can finally resolve your childhood issues if you stay conscious of the process.

In a more general sense, everyone who comes into your life and upsets you in some way is a teacher for you, activating old hurts and unresolved conflicts. You may not see these people as teachers to help you solve your problems, so the opportunity passes you by. I tell my clients and students that "central casting" will keep sending people into their lives to help them resolve these problems as long as they live. When you resolve the old problem brought to you by a certain type of person or situation, "central casting" will stop sending these people or situations to you. Most often, you have conditioned yourself to see yourself as a victim of these people and situations, and you project blame and anger at them instead of receiving their gift. With awareness and new communication skills, you can begin to make new responses to these people and situations that help you in healing your wounds and help promote a "wholeness" to your being.

Basic Needs of Children and Adults

Interestingly, the basic needs of our children and ourselves as adults are not much different. If we understand this fact, it makes it easier for us to understand what children are trying to tell us about their needs. We both need:

1. to have someone understand and respect our needs
2. to have our feelings and needs listened to and taken seriously
3. to have responses from significant others that help validate who we really are
4. to be able to learn from each other

Obviously children need additional physical and emotional support and will have to be "taught" basic living skills, as long as the "teaching methods" do not interfere with those basic needs listed above. In a larger sense, you have much more to learn from your children than you could ever teach them. For example, a child can teach you much more about the nature of feelings than you can learn from adults. In a child, feelings can be observed more clearly because a child expresses his/her feelings much more openly than do adults. You may need to learn how to reconnect with your feelings. By observing children, you can better understand how you got broken so you can fix yourself.

As an adult you are also frequently cut off from your own "inner child," which is the source of your creativity, intuition and vitality. Being with children and observing their play and movements can teach you about how to reconnect with the child within you that you lost contact with somewhere in the process of "growing up."

Because you have this strong yearning to reconnect with the energy of your inner child, as an adult you will unconsciously create situations that help you to begin to make the reconnection. Unfortunately, these often fail to bring the desired result because there is a lack of awareness of how the connection with your inner child was broken or cut off. Also, when a present-day situation resembles a childhood situation in some important way, you may be flooded with repressed feelings stemming from that original childhood situation. These feelings often are very intense, and your natural response may be to push them down again out of a fear that they might overpower

15

you and that you will again have to relive these helpless, awful feelings of childhood. When you push down your natural feelings, you may become "emotionally fixed" back into the original situation and your responses begin to trigger automatically. These automatic responses are wired into your nervous system and require you generally to act one of three ways to this perceived danger: You can either fight, flee or freeze. In either case, you are trapped by these primitive responses and are often unable to make new and conscious responses to a situation that could bring desirable outcomes.

This process occurs frequently in adults who are in relationships. Everyone enters a relationship with a strong yearning for healing and wholing. You hope that relationship will bring you intimacy, understanding, respect, mirroring, touching and trust. You hope that through close relationships you will be able to finally heal the wounds from your childhood and become a whole person. Unfortunately, again because you are really unaware of the dynamic of this process, you end up feeling betrayed and wounded again rather than accomplishing any healing.

Another confusing and frustrating aspect of this process is that the closer you get to another person in a relationship, the more these old patterns will show up. There has to be a certain level of intimacy, closeness and stability to provide the safety for these old patterns to emerge. So in the courting stage of a relationship, the intimacy required to trigger these old responses is only there occasionally. However, when a couple gets married or starts to live together, contact, closeness and stability often activate many of these old patterns. This is probably where the expression "when the honeymoon is over" comes from. This is really what happens and the real purpose of the relationship (still not conscious) takes over. Without a conscious awareness of these healing and wholing purposes of adult relationships, it is impossible for us to utilize our intimate relationships to these ends.

CHAPTER TWO

The Ties That Bind

> When I was a child, I spoke as a
> child ... but
> when I became an adult I put away
> childish things.
> —1 CORINTHIANS: 13

In the previous chapter we began to see how the vicious cycle of cruelty repeats itself in each generation until it is finally broken. We also saw how repression and denial of our true feelings contribute to keeping us stuck in this destructive cycle. This chapter will focus on an overview of the "healing and becoming whole" process of how to identify and break out of these addictive behavior patterns that you unwittingly have brought with you into your adult relationships.

General Family Patterns (Ray 1980)

One of the best ways I have found to help individuals and couples become aware of this healing process is to help them identify the general family patterns that commonly show up in adult relationships. These represent the most unresolved issues from your childhood, and with a new awareness, you can begin to build new perceptions of what really happened to you during childhood. Also you can begin to understand how these patterns are still operating subconsciously in your current relationships. I will list them here briefly and more completely in Chapters 3, 4, 5, 6 and 7 where each one will be presented in detail to help you identify those present in your current relationships.

GENERAL PATTERN 1

Reappearance of Unresolved Parental Traits

What you know about relationships was learned in your relationships either with your parents and other siblings or from other adults such as teachers and family friends. All the attitudes, values, beliefs, feelings and thoughts you have about your current relationships came from these sources and likely were well developed by ten years of age. In an attempt to better understand what really happened to you as a child and what is happening in your current relationships, you may unconsciously recreate as closely as possible in your current relationships the behaviors, attitudes and feelings that as a child you had trouble dealing with in your parents. You tend to selectively perceive these traits in your intimates, co-workers, bosses, etc. For example, if you had a father who had a "bad temper" and you never learned how to cope with his temper as a child, you may see your spouse, boss, co-workers or friends as being "a person with a bad temper just like my father."

GENERAL PATTERN 2

Instant Replay of Co-Dependent Family Relationships

If your relationship with one or both of your parents was full of conflict or confusion and little emotional separateness, you may recreate in your current relationships the same kind of relationship you had with your parents. For example, if you were expected to take care of your parents' feelings by being obedient, thoughtful and subservient to their wishes instead of meeting your own wants and needs, you will find yourself doing the same thing in your adult relationships.

Most children are never given the tools necessary for them to become emotionally separate from their parents, so their most familiar relationship experience is co-dependency. When children physically leave their parents, it is often from a position of counter-dependency ("I'll show you I can make it on my own.") They may still be in this position when they form adult relationships, but they soon fall back into the more familiar co-dependence patterns.

GENERAL PATTERN 3

Living Out Your Parents' Relationship

If your parents' relationship was conflicting or confusing to you, you may try to understand it by recreating in your current relationship the same relationship your parents had with each other. You may find yourself fighting the same way your parents did and maybe even over the same issues, like money, child-rearing and religion. Also, you may still be trying to "fix" your parents' relationship in hopes of finally winning their love, approval or validation of your worth to them.

Specific Family Patterns

Under each of the three most common general family patterns, three specific family patterns are described briefly.

SPECIFIC PATTERN 1a
Parental Disapproval

Under the first general pattern, the unwanted personality traits of your parents tend to show up in current relationships. Specifically, you find that those things your parents disapproved of in you as a child are usually the same things you are "sensitive" about and can easily be hurt by with criticism from those you are close to as adults. Your old "wounds" have not healed, and it seems as if you "draw" people and situations to you in an attempt to finally heal these wounds.

Labels like "selfish" or "unappreciative" may cut deeper because of old hurts related to being seen that way by your parents when you were a child. You may disapprove of yourself in the same way your parents disapproved of you. Also, you may disapprove of the same things in others that your parents disliked. In short, you may hold prejudices, beliefs and values similar to your parents although you may not even be aware of this fact.

SPECIFIC PATTERN 1b
Getting Even

You may find yourself using these same disapproval methods on others who you perceive as weaker than you. In reality this is another way to try to heal your wounds by "acting out" your hurt feelings in front of others. However, the only way these wounds can heal is by *feeling* the feelings and expressing them in more appropriate ways than acting them out, which tends to keep you from your true feelings. You may "blow up" at someone in order to avoid feeling the hurt that you are experiencing.

19

SPECIFIC PATTERN 1c
Self-Condemnation

The other way you act out this first general pattern is by "beating yourself up" by using the same disapproval methods and expressions your parents used on you as a child. Sometimes you may hear yourself criticizing your mistakes, saying almost verbatim what your parents said to you as a child. Have you ever done something embarrassing and then heard yourself calling yourself names such as "stupid" or "you jerk" or some other degrading term that you remember your parents using on you as a child?

SPECIFIC PATTERN 2a
Acting Weak and Helpless

Under the second general pattern, you tend to recreate in the present the same conflictual relationships you had with your parents when you were a child. You may find yourself acting weak and helpless toward your spouse or boss the same way you did toward your mother when you were a child. You may let others take responsibility for your life either because you don't feel able to do it for yourself or because it is easier to blame them if something goes wrong. Many people get "stuck" in infancy and spend the rest of their lives trying to get other people to take care of them. Most alcoholics have this pattern.

SPECIFIC PATTERN 2b
Life Is a Struggle

Because of the struggles you had with your parents while growing up, you may find comfort and familiarity in the struggles in your adult relationships. So when there is an absence of struggle or conflict, you may get anxious and uncomfortable and attempt to create a conflict. It is as though you have become addicted to the drama of struggle and conflict and cannot tolerate peace and harmony in your life.

SPECIFIC PATTERN 2c
Sexual Repression

Another specific issue that falls under this second general pattern is your repressed sexual feelings that can also affect your adult sexuality. Because you are a sexual being, and because in most families sex is never openly discussed, normal sexual feelings between parents and children are never verbally acknowledged. Instead, many parents and other adults "act out" their repressed sexual feelings on their children either overtly or covertly or by rejecting their children when the child begins to develop sexually. As a result, many of you had to repress your sexual feelings as children or were victims of sexual acting out or rejection. Later, your adult relationships involving sex are often profoundly affected by this sexual repression or abuse.

These are the most common causes of impotence and frigidity in men and women and can severely limit your freedom to express your sexual feelings appropriately in your adult relationships. Promiscuous sexual behavior and teenage pregnancies often result from perceived parental rejection.

SPECIFIC PATTERN 3a
The Parentized Child

Under the third general family pattern, you may still be trying to understand the relationship your parents had with each other. If the model you have of a husband/wife or father/mother relationship is one filled with conflict and confusion, you are likely to recreate that pattern unconsciously in all your close relationships as an adult. Unresolved loyalty and legacy issues with your family of origin confuse matters even more. You may feel you owe them great debts that you can only repay by being "loyal" to them and their wishes. Finally, if you remain an extension of your parents' unresolved lives, you can easily become "parentized." You can become an object to be manipulated to satisfy your parents' unmet needs. This pattern must be broken before you can form lasting adult relationships.

SPECIFIC PATTERN 3b
The Fear of Success

If you were raised to take care of your parents' wants and needs first and deny your own wants and needs, you may fear being more successful financially, socially, educationally and psychologically than your parents were or are currently. You may limit yourself and your adult relationships in these ways so as not to "make your parents feel bad or look bad."

SPECIFIC PATTERN 3c
The Fear of the Unknown

Finally, under the influence of this pattern, you may limit your adult relationships just because of a fear of the unknown. If you do "break your family patterns," it means venturing out into unfamiliar waters far beyond those traveled by your parents. Your success in dealing with the unknown will depend partially upon how your parents supported your attempts to explore new and unknown territory. Most parents will encourage and support their children's ventures into new and better ways of relationship. These parents will recognize the limitations that they had to overcome and will want their children to have an easier and happier life. In your innocence, you often expect this kind of love and support from your parents only to be greatly disappointed and confused when they hold on, criticize, control and discourage your efforts to live a freer and happier life, often asking you to live out their fear of the unknown.

As you become aware of these transgenerational patterns, you can begin to see that your parents are (or were) also scared children with unhealed wounds and hurts. You can begin to have compassion for their struggle as people and as parents rather than holding on to resentment and anger over their lack of support. When you can see your parents as they really are and not the idealized way you would like them to be, then you can begin to see yourself and others the way you and they really are. This expanded reality can set you free to grow up and take charge of healing your wounds and finally establishing the loving, effective adult relationships that you have always wanted.

Through a Glass Darkly

Most of you probably cannot remember what really happened to you as a young child. You may remember certain selected events, but chances are that if you compared notes with others who were actually present at these events, they would have a very different story to tell. Actually, stories told by your parents about your childhood serve as the most frequent (although inaccurate) source of information for you. The job of trying to reconstruct what actually happened is almost impossible, but three important facts do help make the task workable.

First, it isn't important that you remember actual events, but it *is* important that you remember the *feelings* that were likely triggered

22

by these actual events. Also, what is important is your *perception* of what happened rather than what actually did happen. *Your feelings are based upon your perceptions of reality and not necessarily reality itself.* Finally, all the information you seek about your past usually is available in your present behavior. The problems and conflicts that show up in your current relationships provide you with strong evidence of what the original situation must have been and how you may have dealt with it originally. Although much has changed in your life, if something has remained unresolved since childhood, it will reappear in an adult form, still attempting to get resolved.

The basic drive of all people is toward wholeness and completion. Anything left incomplete tugs at you to reach completion. If you could but see yourself in a continuous process of moving toward wholeness and completion, you would have the larger context you need to understand all of your behavior. Your attempts at completion often look very self-defeating, but they also tell you where you are stuck in your process of completion. The natural learning style of all human beings is to repeat behaviors until the understanding or awareness is complete. When these unresolved problems and conflicts reappear in your current relationships, they present you with another opportunity to reach completion. One thing you can count on is that *if you don't complete and resolve the problems, they will reappear again and again in your life.*

Some people have suggested that this could be the cause of senility in older people. These people seem to have clear memories of the past, and their present-time thinking is confused and disoriented. It may be that their consciousness is flooded by memories of unresolved issues and feelings, leaving them confused and with little awareness of present-time events. With this sort of flooding of unresolved memories or unresolved issues, it may also be difficult to even distinguish the past from the present time. Those who do therapeutic work with the aged often report significant reduction in behavior that we call senility in those people who do finally resolve some of their problems from the past.

The Body Process

In addition to repeating themselves in present relationships, unresolved issues also tend to create more and more tension in your body the longer they go unresolved. Your repressed feelings are stored as

23

tension in nerves, joints, muscles and organs. When the tension gets great enough, people get sick. This means that your systems are on overload, and there is a breakdown of one or more of the interrelated systems of your body. We use the word *dis-ease* to describe the process when someone gets sick. When a body system breaks down, it is likely to cause permanent damage, known as *dis-ease*. A dis-ease in the body can become acute, chronic or degenerative until, eventually, if the cause of the dis-ease is not found, the body of the person dies or stops functioning altogether. This way of looking at illness and dis-ease is gaining much support even among medically trained people. The American Medical Association is now admitting that as much as 80% of all illness may have a psychological basis or cause. (Ferguson 1980)

This understanding of the causes of dis-ease is beginning to revolutionize the way we treat sick and dying people, and as a result, you may have to unlearn some of your old beliefs as well. For many of us, the germ theory of illness is hard to give up. We were taught to believe that germs invade your body and make you sick. Now we are learning that your psychological state of being has a lot to do with whether or not any of those invaders has any effect on your health. (We will devote much of Chapters 12 and 13 to a closer examination of the specific relationship between your thoughts and feelings, and your proneness toward certain illnesses.)

Getting Stuck in Infancy

By now you may see that the failure to recognize and break with the energy patterns set up in your family of origin really does prevent you from living a healthy, vital life and instead forces you to live a rather limited life of "quiet desperation." Most of us get stuck in infancy and never completely get free enough to achieve our full adult potentials.

Carl Jung wrote about the process of individuation, in which people begin to take charge of their lives. It is a process that often remains dormant until our forties and fifties before we begin to reexamine our unresolved issues. Others have written about the "psychological birth" of humans, which should be completed by age two but is often left incomplete until later life. (Mahler 1968) The truth is that we all have experienced a premature physical birth because evolution has reduced our fetal life to nine months, while full term for humans once was twenty to twenty-two months. (Verney 1981) Unlike some

24

other species, we come into the world rather helpless and unable to take care of ourselves. We are required to be co-dependent with our mother. About the age of fifteen to eighteen months, we are developmentally ready to be born psychologically and should be able to take care of our basic psychological needs, at least at survival level. Most people, however, are not ready at this age or maybe at any other age because they did not receive the psychological tools necessary to achieve their second birth. Our current child-rearing practices do not nurture and support the infant toward the completion of this birth process. So your first attempt at the completion of your most basic process, that of becoming fully human, is thwarted and your development is arrested. This leaves co-dependency as the template for further attempts to break away from the control of the energy patterns of your family of origin and makes the process of individuation or psychological birth a difficult one indeed. In reality, by breaking your family patterns, you are attempting to recover your true self, your psychological heritage that was stifled by your family heritage. Chapter 8 discusses these developmental issues more fully.

The Process of Recovery of Your True Self

The major goal of this book is to teach you how to recover your true self. I will outline this process briefly and then discuss each step more completely. I have seen people who recapitulate much of this whole process in one therapy session, even though I recognize that the process itself can take a lifetime to complete. The process is described as a map and not as the territory, which we must experience in our own unique way. Recovery begins by:

1. Admitting that you are powerless to change your compulsive and addictive behaviors (co-dependency, alcoholism, drug or substance abuse, dysfunctional behavior patterns) without some help. Removing your denial and admitting that you need help is the biggest step in this whole process.

2. Committing yourself to learning to identify the unresolved issues you learned from your family of origin.

3. Learning to recognize your family patterns as they occur in your present relationships.

4. Learning to feel and express completely the repressed and/or denied feelings from your childhood.

5. Developing a new understanding of what really happened to you as a child.

6. Developing new feelings connected to what really happened to you as a child.

7. Learning to take responsibility for your new thoughts and feelings. This means taking charge of your life and no longer expecting someone else to do it for you.

8. Developing a new picture of your family of origin and your role in that family without feelings of hurt or condemnation.

9. Feeling compassion for your parents and for yourself as imperfect human beings.

10. Accepting your parents and yourself just the way that you and they are.

11. Forgiving your parents and yourself. This means to "give back" to them what is rightfully theirs and give back to yourself what is rightfully yours.

12. Restoring the wholeness of your mind, body and spirit through the connection with your true self.

ADMITTING THE PROBLEM—Unless you are willing and able to admit that you cannot control your own life and your compulsive behavior patterns, you will be unable to change your life much at all. Rationalizations, excuses, projections and blaming others all can keep you from admitting the one undeniable fact: your life is not working the way you would like it to work.

COMMITTING YOURSELF TO CHANGE—The best way to start with recognizing your family patterns is to look at your present relationships and begin to notice the issues and problems that seem to come up again and again. If your closest relationships are satisfying and free of conflict or problems, that is a good indication that you have broken free from any of these restrictive patterns. However, it is important to note that the closer you get and the more intimacy you have in your relationships, the more likely these pattern-based problems will surface. This is often very shocking and discouraging to a blissful couple who suddenly find themselves dealing with seemingly monstrous problems. If there are unresolved issues, they will reappear 1) as unwanted parental traits showing up in people you relate to; 2) as similar relationship dynamics between you and those you relate to;

or 3) in the form of relationships that resemble those your parents had with each other.

The three most common ways to notice the presence of these patterns is 1) when you speak of very painful present-time experiences with very little feeling or with apathy, 2) you seem to overreact to a present-time situation by feeling very intense feelings and 3) you tend to idealize your partner or your parents. People who are repressing their feelings react in the first way; people who are overwhelmed by their feelings use the second way; and people who deny their feelings generally use the third way.

EXPRESSING REPRESSED FEELINGS—Most likely you were taught not to express certain feelings in your family of origin. Either you were told directly not to express anger or you were punished severely when you did. Also, you may have seen your parents not expressing their feelings either. This denial and repression of your basic feelings is what keeps you trapped in the childhood pattern.

These feelings may begin to come to the surface as you begin reading parts of this book. I would like to encourage you to let your feelings out. Express them in whatever way you can without hurting yourself or others. Anger is usually one of the first feelings to surface and generally is closer to the surface initially. Yelling while driving (with the windows closed) is a good release. Raging into a tape recorder also can work. The best ways also seem to involve movement. Kneeling and swatting a vinyl beanbag chair or pillow with a tennis racket is a good way because the sound of the racket hitting the vinyl makes a loud, cracking noise. Take the tennis racket in both hands and lift it back over your head, arching your back, and make a sound as you swing down and forward against the vinyl. Also you can use a rolled-up towel to beat on your bed until you get your anger and frustration out.

Create a safe and comfortable situation for yourself where you can really experience complete rage if you have to. Rage and anger usually can be expressed quickly in five or ten minutes, and then they are over. When rage changes to sorrow, it is a good sign that the vicious cycle of cruelty is breaking. If an outburst of anger is followed by grief over having been victimized, then it is also possible to move to the next step where you can actually grieve for your parents who were also victimized. As you learn to feel your pain and sorrow at the way things were, you can then move to more complete and genuine understanding and finally liberation from the effects of these events.

Don't forget that anger is usually a *surface* feeling. Look deeper for sadness, fear, hurt and grief. Most children are not capable of fully expressing these deeper feelings, so almost every adult has unfinished emotional work to do in these areas. If you cry when you hear a sad story or see a movie, these are reminders of uncried tears from your childhood. Most of Chapter 15 will be devoted to ways of releasing repressed feelings.

REEDUCATING THE CHILD WITHIN—This requires you to develop a new picture of what really happened to you as a child. Expressing the feeling required in the previous step usually opens up space for this. It also means developing new feelings connected to this picture. You may need to focus your negative emotional energy at your mother and your father. Take them one at a time and act as their prosecutor.

One form of reeducation I use is asking people to write a Negative Emotional Autobiography (form given in Chapter 16) documenting all the negative experiences and feelings you remember encountering with each parent. This includes documenting the incidents and your feelings when your parents were indifferent to your true feelings, unable to see or respect you, or saw you as a burden, etc. The purpose of this activity is to purge all your negative feelings in order to open the channels to make room for new feelings and awarenesses. The second part of this reeducation involves beginning to see your parents more clearly as people who because of their programming were unable to respond differently to you. Again I often ask people to write out their defense and, by having them read it aloud or even act it out, it is easy to tell whether or not the process is working for them.

If they are having trouble mounting a defense, it indicates a need for more prosecution. Some people need many rounds of this prosecution and defense before some new, more positive and loving feelings begin to emerge. This part of the process involves fighting the inner war with yourself. By now, your intellectual part probably can look more objectively at what happened to you in childhood, but the negative emotional part still has to be satisfied. This involves an inner dialogue between these two parts. Each gets a turn to bitch at the other for a while. Then the two parts are allowed to work through their conflict and reach an agreement on how to deal with the needs of each. A plan for carrying that out is made and tested. Revisions are made based upon our experience using the plan.

TAKING RESPONSIBILITY FOR YOUR LIFE—This is the point in the process where a major shift has to occur. You have to take full responsibility for your life if you haven't by now. No longer can you look for anyone to blame or to take responsibility for you. From this point on, you must realize that you are the only person responsible for your life. If *you* don't fix what got broken, it won't get fixed.

FEELING COMPASSION—Genuine compassion and understanding can only be learned by clearing out the negative mass stored in your body. When you can truly get angry at your parents and get it out of your system, a sense of loving them comes into your awareness. The cloud of negativity lifts and you can see your parents' true nature as well as your own.

ACCEPTANCE—True acceptance of your parents as people with problems and potentials often leads to an equal acceptance of yourself as you really are. You will find that the hardest part of the process is self-acceptance. This is an important step in the process of recovering your true self.

FORGIVENESS—This means to give back to your parents and to your true self that which belonged to each. In growing, you mistakenly took on some of your parents' beliefs, behaviors, attitudes, prejudices and feelings. By now, in the process of recovery of your true self, you should be able to sort out what is yours and what belongs to your parents. True forgiveness can only come if you can feel outraged at the injustices you have endured and can recognize the lies they told you and can feel hateful toward your parents for what they did to you. This kind of forgiveness can't be dictated or rehearsed. It comes spontaneously as an act of grace that shifts your whole perceptual world on its axis. You are changed, transformed, by your ability to express and acknowledge even your ugliest and most forbidden thoughts and feelings.

RECONNECTION WITH YOUR TRUE SELF—Finally you are free of the negative mass that was stuck in your body and energy systems. You can now truly find your place in the sun and begin to fulfill your birthright as a full human being. You are then free to pursue a relationship to its fullest, at all levels.

Awareness Activity

The following awareness activity is intended to help you focus on what it feels like to begin to reconnect with your true self. Either read the following essay aloud while facing yourself in the mirror, or sit with your eyes closed and ask someone close to you to read it to you.

Every relationship begins with your relationship with and empathy for yourself and sets the foundation for all your other relationships. In our preoccupation with others, we often forget that the basis of every loving relationship is our loving relationship with our *Self*.

It seems to be a paradox of our human existence that the degree to which we can love another human being corresponds directly with our ability to love and affirm our Self. Only when we are able to love our Self can we truly love another person and risk being self-less in that relationship.

Our societal/cultural/family experiences all tell us that to love ourselves is to be selfish. Actually, selfishness is the very opposite of self-love or selfness. The purpose of this activity is to help you learn to reconnect with your true inner Self where your love and your power are integrated naturally. This process starts by asking you to adopt a kindly, accepting, positive attitude toward your true Self. Most people feel they really do love themselves, but deep down the exact opposite may be true. We may be afraid to confront/explore, in an understanding and loving manner, those areas of ourselves that we fear. Carl Jung once said that "the least of my brethren is me!"

Imagine for a moment (either with your eyes closed or facing yourself in the mirror) that you are another person, someone you truly love. (If your eyes are closed, imagine this person, you, sitting right in front of you.) Look yourself right in the eyes and begin to ask yourself the following questions; then wait for the honest answer to come to you: Do I really try to recognize, accept and respect this person's feelings—honestly? . . . Am I aware of this person's gifts, talents and exciting potential? . . . Am I aware of this person's limitations, and am I willing to learn

30

from these mistakes and failures rather than be crushed by them? . . . Am I able to really listen to this person, to the feelings, insights and intuitions? . . . Do I pay attention to this person's body and its needs as well as what promotes its wellness? . . . Can I play with this body and am I aware of all the ways I can express my love to it? . . . Do I recognize this person as a gift—a cause of celebration—seeing him or her truly and clearly? . . . Do I still recognize the holes, the brokenness and incompleteness as well? . . . Can I forgive this person? . . . Am I willing to think of this person as gently and lovingly as the other people that I love?

By asking you to focus on yourself in this way, I am not asking you to become self-centered or totally preoccupied with yourself. I am asking you to develop a balance so you can show the same loving concern for yourself that you can show to a "neighbor" or to those you love most.

If you begin to do this, you know what it means, don't you? It means that you will have to continue to look at yourself in loving ways, and that may take courage because you will also see the parts of you that are hardest to love. You may see your evil, your impatience, your greed, your jealousy, your pessimism, your unkindness and your fear. And then, when you get over the horror of all that, and can face *all* of you, you will have power—the greatest power, really. The truth will set you free—it brings even more love. Because if you can see yourself as you really are—and love it *all*—then you can begin to accept and love and affirm this reality in others. By denying your faults and limitations, you only strengthen their hold on you and make yourself feel more powerless and less loving. By recognizing and accepting your weaknesses, you take away the poison and you destroy their hold on you.

The feeling of being in love with your true Self doesn't imply that you have risen above all your faults and emotional problems. It merely implies that you refuse to be paralyzed by them. When you realize this, you are free to love yourself and others without strings, games, fears or exploitation. Then you can begin to truly rejoice in and celebrate your own uniqueness and goodness. You can go now into the world carrying with you a deep sense of freedom and peace.

CHAPTER THREE

Reappearance of Unwanted Parental Traits

Life only demands from you the strength you possess; only one feat is possible—not to have run away.
—DAG HAMMARSKJÖLD, *MARKINGS*

How to Recognize Family Patterns in Current Relationships

The quickest and easiest way to recognize when these old family patterns are operating is to pay attention to your basic senses. When old, unresolved issues surface, your senses will become activated, usually sending out stronger signals than the situation actually calls for. You can recognize unresolved family patterns when: there is a lump in your throat, an edge in your voice; you feel a sinking feeling or a flooding of feelings in your body; you see actual images of previous times when you felt this way; you recall familiar smells and tastes; you experience a rush of adrenalin in your bloodstream that signals danger, even though the situation doesn't appear that dangerous.

Another way to recognize the presence of these patterns is when you feel stuck with only one way to respond to a situation. It is as though you are "fused" back into the original situation and can only see one way of dealing with it, which is usually the way you dealt with it in the original situation. These mixed and double signals always indicate the presence of old patterns and unresolved issues from your past. You can come to recognize these signals and learn ways to process the signals to find out what the old issue is. Or you can learn ways to communicate to others what is happening and ask for their help in sorting out the issues. When two people in a committed relationship agree to help each other with this process, it can lead to a healing of old wounds and a resolution of these recurring issues. The process of uncovering these patterns and working on them with a cooperative partner can be quite exciting and rewarding rather than frightening and frustrating. I must warn you, however, that the process is usually a slow one requiring patience and perseverance.

My experience has been that even when a couple is working together cooperatively on these issues, it can still take several years to uncover and work through the major patterns and unresolved issues. In relationships where your partner is resistant, or if you are not currently in a committed relationship, the process can take much longer, perhaps three to five years or more. This also seems to depend upon the age at which you start the process. One rule of thumb: Realize that to become conscious enough to achieve positive results, the process takes about one month for every year you have been alive. So a thirty-year-old starting the process can figure that about thirty months of work on his or her patterns will be necessary to bring enough of them into conscious awareness to begin to produce lasting changes.

In addition, when you work through one pattern, another deeper one may then appear, which requires you to start over again with the new pattern until that pattern is broken, only to have yet another pattern then appear. In short, I believe that this is a lifetime process, and the more patterns you break the freer you will become in your life. This may seem like a long time to work on these patterns, but the rewards that come from this work make it worth it. As one client stated, "I felt like I was living in a fog where I couldn't seem to prevent these awful feelings and events from occurring. Now I can see and feel things coming up and know what to do to deal with them." Another said, "I used to be someone who had bad things happen to him, and now I am in a place where I am someone who can make good things happen for myself."

Gail Sheehy in her book *Passages* (1976) says that when we discover we are in charge of our lives, ". . . we no longer have to ask permission because we are the providers of our own safety." You are

33

now in touch with your own internal power and no longer have to rely on any external power to tell you how to run your life. The opposite of living a life dominated by these patterns is not a life of gaiety characterized by an absence of pain or problems. It is a life full of vitality where you can experience life fully and feel all of your feelings directly, from intense love and joy to envy, jealousy, rage, grief, despair and mourning. From this conscious place, you can create new and more functional patterns for your life.

Also, as you understand the flow and process of changing these patterns, you never have to be stuck in a pattern again. You can become aware of a pattern that was once very functional and see it as having outlived its function, now in need of being changed. In this way you can become a co-creator with nature or the universal flow or whatever you want to call the natural process that impels you to move forward toward wholeness or completeness.

GENERAL PATTERN 1
Dealing With Unwanted Parental Traits

In order to develop your awareness of the presence of these patterns in your life, the description of each general pattern and each specific sub-pattern will have a written awareness activity connected to it to help you personalize the information.

Awareness Activity:
Identifying Parental Traits

Step One: Make a list of traits to describe your mother and another list of traits to describe your father. These lists can either be as you see them now or as you remember them from childhood. If you were raised by someone other than your biological parents, use them instead. Use the persons who functioned in the parenting role most of the time you were growing up, including older siblings who may have been surrogate parents for you. You should be able to list at least ten separate traits for each parent. (If you have trouble listing ten traits for either parent, that would suggest the lack of a strong or close relationship with that parent. Sometimes a parent is absent from the home due to job or illness, and that prevented you from developing a close relationship with this person.)

Step Two: Read over your two lists and place a check mark next

34

to those traits that you identify with in yourself. You likely will find that many traits you saw in your parents are present in yourself. You may have found it easier to identify with the traits of one parent and not the other. This could relate to the strength of the relationship or it could relate to unresolved conflicts in your relationship with that parent. For example, if you didn't identify any, or listed only a few traits of your father, you may be denying those qualities in yourself; or, if you only selected positive traits to identify, you may be blocking out unwanted traits in both of you.

Step Three: Those traits you didn't identify with may be projected onto others in your life. Place the initials of the person next to each parental trait that you see in others. This will help you see onto whom you tend to project these traits.

Step Four: A way to further refine this process is to complete the following chart:

	POSITIVE	NEGATIVE
Ways I am like my Mother/Father		
Ways I am not like my Mother/Father		

DISCUSSION OF RESULTS IN STEP FOUR—There are several ways to interpret the results. The best results would be a distribution of traits in each cell of the chart. First, look for any blank cells in the upper half of the chart. This would be evidence of some possible denial or blocking. For example, if I only identified with the positive traits of my father and no negative traits, I may have a distorted picture of him as a person. Sometimes people see one parent as all negative and the other as all positive, which is usually a distortion of the way they really are, but important to be aware of. It may signal a tendency to split the world into categories of good and bad and indicate a problem seeing people or events with mixed traits. An empty cell in the lower half of the chart could indicate a blind spot in your self-awareness or a lack of differentiation between you and your parent.

One woman who could not list any ways she was not like her mother said, "When I look in the mirror I see my mother." In her case, she had no problem identifying the ways she was like her mother, but she did not have a clear picture of herself as someone separate from her parent. This is particularly true if when you were a child you had to deny yourself and your needs in order to meet parental wishes and expectations. Actually, this is how you lost sight of your true self and your own identity. You put on a false self and tried to be more like them or to be the way they wanted you to be. You may have reasoned that if you were only more like them or more like they wanted you to be, then they would treat you better or love you more. In most cases, trying to be like them backfires because, unknown to you, your parents probably didn't like *themselves* very much.

A friend told me a story that illustrates this point. It is about a family he knew in which the daughter could never get her parents' approval of the men she dated. Finally she thought she had found a man that they approved of and announced to them that she was going to get married to him. At this announcement, her parents became furious at her and began to criticize this man as lazy, unstable, unfeeling and irresponsible. To these criticisms, all she could use to defend her choice was to exclaim in tearful frustration, "But Daddy, he is so much like you!"

WHAT YOU RESIST WILL PERSIST—The basis for the persistent reappearance of these traits in our relationships is the old adage that "what you resist is what persists." If you have resisted looking at an unresolved problem from childhood, hoping it would go away when you grew up and left home, you are often shocked to see the problem reappear in your current relationships. This may be even more shocking if you thought you were deliberately choosing a partner who didn't have the unwanted traits that your parents may have had.

Actually, one of three or four different alternative processes may have been going on without your conscious knowledge.

1. Despite the conflicts, you are attracted to someone who is like the parent with whom you had greatest conflict. You may see only the positive similarities at first, and perhaps you think you can solve the original problem by having a successful relationship with someone

36

who is like your mother or father. That may also reinforce your fantasy belief that the problem was really his or her fault anyway.

2. You may also interpret the behavior of your current partner as being like that of a parent with whom you had a conflict. The motive behind this kind of selective perception is usually: Maybe you can better understand your parent through your current relationship. This usually is accompanied by an unspoken demand that your partner cooperate in your learning experiment, which he or she will seldom do unless you ask them directly and they agree.

3. You may finally try to find someone who you think is exactly the opposite in personality to the parent with whom you had trouble. The hope is that this way you can avoid ever having to deal with the problem again. This can work for a while, but you can become too uncomfortable with the unfamiliar and unconsciously begin to put pressure on the person *to become more like the conflictual parent.* You may not like the conflicts, but you like the unfamiliar even less.

4. You become like the parent with whom you had trouble dealing. This "identification with the aggressor" alternative may be related to your need for revenge in the vicious cycle of cruelty, or it could also be a way you think you can better understand this person with whom you couldn't deal. You may believe that if you only were better able to understand him or her, you could then learn to deal with his bad temper or her over-protectiveness.

SPECIFIC PATTERN 1a
Parental Disapproval

Awareness Activity

Make a list of at least five things your mother disapproved of in you as a child, and at least five things your father disapproved of in you as a child. After you complete the two lists, go back and place a check mark (√) next to those things you now disapprove of in yourself and an (x) next to those you now disapprove of in others.

DISCUSSION OF RESULTS—You should see some similar pattern here either in your self-disapproval or in your disapproval of others or in both. What seems to happen to you without your awareness is that you take on your parents' beliefs, values and prejudices. You particularly tend to disapprove of those things in others that your parents

37

disapproved of in you. Also, you are most affected by the disapproval of others that resembles in content or form your parents' disapproval of you. If your parents disapproved of idleness and called you "lazy" or "worthless" when you were idle, you now may project that label on others, as well as be very sensitive to and easily hurt by even an implied statement regarding a lack of industry on your part. The truth is that you often disapprove of yourself in much the same way. You beat yourself up, often with the exact words and phrases that your parents used on you.

Since most of your values and beliefs were formed before age ten, you likely had not developed enough independent thinking processes by that age to help you decide whether or not what they said was true. So you believed that your all-knowing parents were right and you deserved to be criticized or disapproved of. This made it even harder to tell them about your hurt feelings and the woundings to your self-esteem that occurred as a result of their criticism. One woman said to me, "Whenever I express myself, I am afraid of disapproval; I'm afraid that people won't like me. I place other people's opinion ahead of my own, thinking that *they* know the right answer."

In addition, behind this sensitivity are unintegrated hurt feelings at being called names or at having had these beliefs forced upon you as children. To cover up and deny these powerful feelings, you may take on the same belief and inflict it upon yourself and others in much the same way it was inflicted upon you. This serves to help you avoid the deep hurt feelings and helps you to project the disapproval on others in an attempt to discharge some of the emotional energy in a safer way. If I can be mad at you for doing something wrong, it keeps me from being mad at myself for doing the same thing that my parents told me was wrong.

SPECIFIC PATTERN 1b
Getting Even

Again make two lists. One list is headed by "I resent my mother for . . ." A second list is titled, "I resent my father for . . ." While a third list could be "I resent my partner for . . ." A comparison of the lists may help you identify specific issues. If you find that one of the most effective ways for you to avoid your own hurt feelings is by "blowing up" at someone else, you can easily get caught in the pattern of getting even. An excessive focus on the behavior of others is a compulsive way to avoid looking at yourself. I often ask my clients and students the following question: "If someone else other than you were born into your family at the same time you were, is it likely that your parents would have treated this person the same way they treated you?" If the answer is "yes," then you don't need to take what your parents did so personally. They would have done the same to anybody in that position.

NARCISSISTIC WOUNDS—One of the basic reasons why you did take it personally is that at an early age your normal, healthy, narcissistic needs were not allowed to be expressed. You were born needing to be noticed, understood, taken seriously and mirrored by adults. The mirroring process means that when you were held as an infant, you could see yourself mirrored or reflected back in your father's or mother's face. Unfortunately, instead of mirroring you, they projected their own expectations, fears and plans for you, and as a result you did not learn who you really were. Instead you learned to be who your parents wanted you to be. If they expected you to be quiet and not cause any problems, you may not have learned how to identify your own feelings and wishes, and instead you may have stayed focused on the feelings and wishes of those around you.

Your parents were unable to mirror for you because they, too, never got their narcissistic needs met as a child and felt resentful. If they saw you trying to get these needs met, they would likely get angry or feel as though it wasn't fair that you could get these needs met and they couldn't. What they were unable to find in their parents, they now wanted to find in their children. Finally they had someone who would be completely centered on them and not abandon them.

Children are often used in this way to fulfill these unmet needs in their parents. This is especially true if you were the first born, an only child or the last born. In some families, all the children are subjected to this repression in service of the needs of the parents. In other families, one child, usually the first-born child, becomes the one on whom the parents focus. In some cases where children are raised by a grandmother or nurse, they can escape the tyranny of a narcissistically deprived mother enough to develop their own internal connections.

This lack of mirroring can easily get passed from one generation to the next without any notice. The result of a lack of mirroring is that unconsciously you search for this mirroring in your close adult relationships and, when you don't find it, you may even change partners, get a divorce or leave a partner. The other common way to try to get these needs met is by having children and using them as objects of your own narcissistic search.

A female client once said to me, "I felt loved and wanted, like an object, a doll. I was dressed up and pampered and treated like a princess. There was no 'self' there, just someone who mechanically did 'child-like' things." You remember your narcissistic wounds each time you seek this mirroring and do not find it. These are memories of deep feelings of sadness and hurt that you are protecting with your ego defense mechanisms. In addition, you may have been conditioned to respond to external stimuli and not internal ones, so you may not even be aware of your deep feelings. Your children do provide you with many opportunities to deal with your narcissistic wounds. When you are able to really empathize with your children when they are feeling defenseless, hurt or humiliated, you will also see your childhood pain. Some people have to turn away from this pain, while others can look and feel sad for their children and for themselves. When you do not turn away, you can learn more about your behavior than you will ever learn from a book.

GRANDIOSITY AND DEPRESSION: THE DOUBLE-EDGED SWORD—The two main response patterns that people with unmet narcissistic needs have are 1) being grandiose, requiring constant admiration and approval or 2) being depressed, also requiring constant admiration and approval. Behind both is a compulsion to fulfill the expectations of parents and others. The grandiose person temporarily feels successful, and the depressed person temporarily feels unsuccessful, at meeting these internalized parental standards. In both cases there is a tremendous fear of failure and of loss of love, very high standards of performance, lack of confidence to risk new things, oversensitivity, lots of guilt and shame, and a denial of unwanted feelings.

SPECIFIC PATTERN 1c
Self-Condemnation
The interesting thing is that when you grow up and move away from your parents, you often find yourself using their actual words to "beat

yourself up" and keep yourself prisoner to their standards instead of developing your own. You deliver to yourself the same blows to your self-esteem that you experienced from your parents. Many times because of guilt and self-hatred, you may also use your body (looking for imperfections), your career (comparing yourself with someone who is more successful), your mate (pushing them away because you feel unworthy), your finances (not making enough money) or your car (not taking care of it and having it break down). In other words, you mess up one or all of these situations to punish yourself for something. You may find yourself filled with guilt, which is actually a fear of punishment. This self-condemnation is often deep and goes back to early childhood or birth. I know of people who felt guilty that they were born, thinking they had caused their parents so much pain (they may have heard stories about how much pain their mother had during childbirth).

Another way people continue to beat themselves up for past wrongdoings is by denying themselves any pleasure and never letting themselves get what they want. Instead, they are likely to become a martyr in the hope that if they suffer long enough, God or some kind soul will absolve them of their guilt. Some people develop chronic pain in their body to help remind them of their guilt.

Much of your social training is responsible for this because you were told more often what you did "wrong" than what you did "right." If you did it right no one ever noticed. As a result, you have much more information about how others see your negative traits (negative mirroring) than you do about how others see your good qualities. You can probably make a longer list of your negative qualities than of your positive qualities.

As one client put it,

> My parents regarded me as basically bad, so they had to beat me
> to teach me how to be good. I remember a couple of times when
> my mother was in an uncontrollable rage over something I did,
> and she was spanking me with a wooden spoon on my bottom.
> She always said, 'This hurts me more than you.' I didn't believe
> her because she was using a wooden spoon to keep her hand from
> hurting. The way I think she meant that was it hurt her to see
> herself be so angry—that was unacceptable to her. After those
> beatings I used to go to my room and hit my doll, Molly, and tell

41

her it hurt me more than it hurt her. It did hurt me more because
I felt guilty for hitting my doll and often I cried and felt awful for
doing that.

Awareness Activity:
Your Personal Law

If you remember the negative things you say to yourself when you
are condemning yourself, there is usually one bottom-line statement
that you will find yourself using over and over. This is the most persistent negative thought you have about yourself. In this awareness
activity, you need to first identify this negative thought. Write it in a
sentence starting with "I . . ." (Example: "I am a worthless person. I
don't deserve to live," or, "I am . . . (not good enough to succeed, to
be liked, etc.)."

After you have written this sentence, list everything you can
think of that you think makes this statement true. Notice any images
and feelings that come to you as you list your negative qualities. Try
to imagine where you got these. Notice which parent gave you the
most of these. Now take each one of these negative traits and imagine
how your life would be different if that were no longer true for you.

If the way your life would be different is something you would
find pleasing, then cross that trait off your list, until you have gone
through every negative trait on your list. This is a way to give back
(for-give) anything you no longer want or need. You may find it
too uncomfortable to give back all these traits, but even if you let
go of a few you may see positive results, and then try letting go of
some more.

The final part of this process involves you in writing a new personal law that is the opposite of the first one you wrote. For example,
you might now write "I am a worthwhile person and I deserve to
live." After writing this very positive sentence (*without* qualifiers like
sometimes, usually or mostly), begin to list all the positive qualities
you have that make this statement true for you. Finally, ask yourself:
"If I believed this were true of me, what changes could I make in my
life?" The answers to this question might show you the possibilities for
a new self-image based not upon parental expectations but upon your
own standards for what *you* want for your life.

Instant Replay of Co-dependent Family Relationships

Most of us become parents
long before we have stopped being
children

—MIGNON MCLAUGHLIN

Three Ways Co-dependent Patterns Get Established

Again it is important to remember that any co-dependent relationship problem from earlier in your life will show up in your current relationships. There also seems to be a kind of "Murphy's Law" at play here. The problem will usually show up when the relationship is close enough to create enough safety for the issue to reappear. The safer and closer your relationships become, the more likely that anything unresolved will raise its ugly head and press for resolution. If you know this is what usually happens, you may avoid thinking you are going crazy or becoming neurotic or that your relationship is falling apart. Many a couple has had this "curse" from the past appear in their relationship, not knowing where it came from, why it was there or what to do about it.

First, be assured that every couple that ever had a close relationship has had to deal with this dragon, but we sure wouldn't know that from the popular literature about relationships. The movies, self-help books, romance novels, advice to the lovelorn columns and the like all seem to be suggesting that these things shouldn't happen to good people and if they do happen to you, there is something wrong with your relationship and with you as an individual. Nothing could be further from the truth, because the natural learning style of human beings *requires* that these issues come to the surface to be dealt with in the safest situations available to you.

Because of the misinformation you have about relationships, you tend to see these unresolved issues as attacks on your well-being and happiness, so you defend against them with all your might. To recognize them as occurring within a natural, normal context in a relationship may help you to deal with the unresolved issues without taking it so personally. Before we go on with ways of dealing with these patterns, let's take a look at some of the main ways these patterns can get established in your family of origin.

The Rebel, the Conformer and the Loner

THE REBEL. In your family of origin there was likely one child who, perhaps because of the accident of birth, was targeted for criticism and abuse more than the other children. This child usually fought the system and resisted the co-dependency and control more than the other children. Because of his personal strength, he was somehow able to maintain his free will and resist all attempts to get him to conform. This does not mean, however, that this child gets away from the family without conflicts. In fact, these children usually have the most conflicts and have to pay a real price, while the other siblings may just conform or withdraw from their real needs and feelings. However, in their fighting to remain free of the domination, rebels often learn quite a bit and perhaps remain closer to their true self than their brothers and sisters who went along with the family pattern or withdrew into themselves.

The price the rebel has to pay is that he or she is often labeled sick, crazy or stupid by his/her parents and other family members. They are the ones who are sent to psychiatrists and psychologists to get "straightened out." In addition, they are also the object of envy of their other siblings who wish they were strong enough to break out of the system. The parents often feel they have to make an example of the non-conforming child for fear the other children will follow the non-conforming example rather than the one they have dictated. The rebel who maintains free will under those conditions will have a number of battle scars and wounds to heal in adult relationships. He or she is likely to be very scared of close relationships and fear being controlled, being vulnerable or getting hurt again.

44

Frequently, the rebels had the most conflictual relationship with the stronger of the two parents who fought them, but frequently they are also angry at the other parent who remained in the background and didn't give any support to them. They may feel more betrayal by the non-dominating parent because at least in the battle with the dominating parent, they got more contact and clarity. The kind of relationship issues that a rebel might have in adult relationships would include fear of closeness, fear of rejection and fear of being hurt again, *but* it always would be covered over by a layer of combative anger.

These kinds of people may be so good at disguising their hurt and fearful feelings that even those close to them may not see their deeper, feeling side very often. In addition, they are often cut off from their own feeling side, defending themselves against the pain and hurt and sadness by being hard, cold and tough. One such person was Hank, who is now thirty years old.

I can never remember my father touching me when I was young. He kept me at a distance and often talked to me as if I was someone sitting next to him at the board meeting of the corporation he ran. By the time I was twelve, I had tried everything I could think of to get any positive love and attention from my father. I was a "straight A" student and was a highly ranked tennis player. The straight A's were what he expected, and he discounted my tennis ability because his game was golf. I became the best pitcher in the county on my little league team, but I gave that up because he wouldn't even come to watch me play.

During this time in the late 1960s we were living in New York, so I had easy access to the counter-culture. The length of my hair became the first way I could get to him. I was delighted that he even noticed me. From then on, I learned many ways to push his buttons: by attending peace marches, rock concerts and hanging out with flower children.

By the time I was sixteen I was rebelling openly. I hated him so much that my responses to everything he stood for, said or did was a screaming "fuck you." He was a real hypocrite. His medicine cabinet was full to the brim with uppers for waking up and downers for sleeping, while during the day he would down two to three quarts of Canadian Club whiskey. It was no surprise to me when one evening he arrived at the door of my room with various drug education pamphlets which linked long hair and incense burning to marijuana smoking and certain heroin addiction.

He began to lecture me incessantly on the evils of non-prescription drugs. Once when he was especially drunk, I said something to him that caused him to take a swing at me. I blocked the punch with my arm and punched him in the chest, breaking several of his ribs.

The next morning I awoke to the sight of four policemen around my bed who, without explanation, put me into a straight-jacket, locked me into a squad car and drove me straight to the local mental institution. As the door of the institution locked behind me, I noticed one woman in a corner putting out a cigarette on the side of her face and another woman defecating uncontrollably while walking across the floor. I knew what I was facing when they threw me into a room with bars on the window and a door with a slot at the bottom to pass food in. There was a bucket in the corner for a toilet and an uncovered mattress on the floor. This is where I spent the next nine months of my life.

I demanded to see a lawyer, my mother or someone—*any-one* —who would explain what was happening. I refused to answer their ridiculous questions about ink blots and how much I masturbated, so they said I was obviously insane. They administered drugs to keep me a zombie, and periodically they gave me shock treatments, about seven or eight all together. There were beatings and other attempts to break my spirit, but everything made me more determined than ever that if I survived this ordeal I would never again let anyone put a wall between me and my freedom.

After I got out, because they couldn't prove insanity, it took some time to get over the drugs they forced me to take and to adjust to the free world again. I was angry and bitter at my parents for leaving me there. They divorced shortly after that, and I spent several years traveling around the world studying with various spiritual groups and teachers, trying to find some meaning in all this. I have had almost no contact with my father, whose business eventually failed. Later he remarried and started living off the money left in a trust for me by my grandfather. To this day I haven't seen one penny of the money from that trust while my father lives lavishly off it. I hate that man, but I still have hope to find some way to make peace with him.

THE CONFORMER. Another common reaction to family patterns is to give in and become co-dependent rather than fight. These are the children who give up their own ideals in favor of their parents' wishes.

They conform to parental wishes and hope that by cooperating, they will be liked or treated better than the rebel. Frequently, this kind of person has very low awareness of his or her own needs and wants. These people are active and appear loving but they often feel very little love either for themselves or others. They tend to agree and follow all the rules, usually not giving their parents much trouble. They receive lots of praise for being good and usually don't explore much on their own. They are often highly dependent upon the praise of parents and teachers and are easily crushed by any negative remark.

In adult relationships, these people continue trying to please in order to earn love and are often disappointed when they can't get others to pay attention to them. With little self-esteem in reserve, these people often have rapid mood swings. When they are getting the praise they want, everything looks wonderful, but that usually doesn't last because something unexpected happens to upset the apple cart and then they are really down on themselves for not performing up to standards.

These people are always trying to meet the standards set by others and feel good when they meet the standards and bad when they don't. Their dependency on others for their well-being is a source of great discomfort, but usually they just try harder. They resent the fact that they let others direct their lives, but they don't feel strong enough to direct it themselves. While they may not have had many actual conflicts with their parents, they do have many unresolved issues with authority and control in relationships. These people may have been spoiled by their parents but in a controlling way, so they would like to be catered to in a close relationship but fear the control that comes with it.

Ann's story illustrates this pattern.

I was the oldest child but I always had the feeling my dad wanted a boy. I never was sure I was seen. When my brother came along, I could tell they treated him differently. He could do more things than I ever could, and I was told by my father that my brother was smarter than me although I never believed it. I really tried hard to earn their approval. I remember making a conscious effort at age eleven to say 'Yes, ma'am,' rather than 'I am.' I had learned that obedience brought approval.

I was the perfect student in school, always trying to give the right answers. I was not given reasons for rules and I don't think I

47

even asked. I was told to do it because they said so. I believed
they knew what was right for me. To this day, whenever I express myself, I'm afraid someone will disapprove of what I have
to say and won't like me. I constantly place other people's opin-
ions before my own. I think that they must know the right
answer.

I always placed my thoughts and needs and feelings second
to someone else's—my brother's, my parents', even my playmate's. I was actually told that I had to learn to like everything
and everyone and was called silly or stupid if I didn't.

As a result of all this, I grew up as *their* child. I did what
they told me to do. I didn't even realize that it was possible to
exist separate from them. Now I feel dependent in my relationships, and every time I act on my own behalf I feel guilty. I resent my husband because he expects me to do everything for him,
and then I forget one thing and he yells at me. I have trouble
with sex, too. It's hard for me to relax and let go. Being sexy is
like being a hooker. Good girls can't be sexy. I'm highly critical of
my body and I'm afraid that my husband is going to criticize me
for being too fat or something. Sex is fascinating to me, but to feel
sexual at all I have to have several drinks. My husband reminds
me of my mother mostly, but sometimes my father as well. I wish
I knew what I really wanted.

THE LONER. The third common reaction to our family patterns was
to withdraw as much as possible from the mainstream of the family.
The goal of the loner is to become invisible and blend into the wood-
work. This person often has no close relationship with either parent
and lives in a shell. These people often have very stiff bodies and
often describe themselves as feeling dead inside. Because they failed
to develop close relationships with their parents, they often lack the
necessary skills to form relationships at all. They are loners, but because they never learned how to become emotionally independent
they, too, have latent co-dependent patterns. They are often very
much cut off from their feelings, too, and take a very rational approach to everything.

These people feel very much unseen by their parents who
were likely too busy anyway to see the hurts and the struggles
the child had. These children just give up and decide it is easier
not to try.

John's story fits this pattern.

48

I always seemed to be disappointed. If I expected something good would happen, it never did. I never seemed to be asked or told about things. I was powerless to change things anyway. They always did what they wanted to do and I just went along for the ride. I learned that my feelings were not very important. If I expressed any feelings, I was told to keep quiet or I was ignored. I felt like they had so many problems of their own that I shouldn't bother them with mine too. My mother nagged at me a lot, always reminding me to do something she had told me to do. I felt like she was saying I wasn't capable of doing it on my own without being reminded.

My dad was another problem. One of the things I disliked the most about my childhood was the sound of my dad's truck coming up the driveway. I never knew what had gone wrong, but I knew that whatever went wrong during his day at work would somehow be my fault and I could get yelled at or punished. Eventually, I developed a keen sense of hearing and, at the first sound of his truck coming up the street, I would stop whatever I was doing and quickly hide in the hills around my house until I could find out what the situation was. If I didn't hear my dad calling for me, I knew that the coast was clear and I could come back home again. Until a few years ago, every time I saw my father my first thought was that I had done something wrong.

I also really feel inadequate around women most of the time. I'm always so afraid of saying or doing the wrong thing that I freeze. I am all thumbs when women are around. I would like to have closer relationships with women but it all seems too hard. Maybe I'll get married someday but my prospects sure don't look good.

All three of these reactions to family socialization contain the major unresolved relationship patterns with your parents that often continue into adulthood. *These addictive reactions form the way you deal with your adult relationships.* All of them limit the amount of true intimacy you can experience in adult relationships. The rebel fears the control that intimacy may bring, the conformer fears the freedom that intimacy brings and the loner fears the unknown that closeness brings. All three are trapped into repeating co-dependent patterns of relationships until they can identify their true feelings and express them in ways they failed to as children. With the *expression* of repressed or denied feelings can come the energy to break the co-dependent patterns and find new and more satisfying ways of relating.

CHAPTER FIVE

Dealing with Co-dependent Family Relationships

The second half of a man's life is made up of nothing but the habits he has acquired during the first half.

—FEODOR DOSTOYEVSKY,
THE BROTHERS KARAMAZOV

GENERAL PATTERN 2
Learning to Deal with Co-dependent Family Relationships

When dealing with these recurrent patterns, it is important to remember that partners play an important role in helping to bring the pattern to your awareness. They are usually unwilling to let you continue being unconscious about the pattern. They often see what is going on before you do, and you may resent their insight or knowledge. Ask yourself, "How come they see this in me and others don't? I thought I had hidden it much better than that. Maybe I can talk them out of it. Because if I can't, I may have to change and risk feeling that old pain again." You may also fear that they are going to reject you if you really admit to a problem. Frequently, you begin to see them in a parental way with power over you, and your favorite way of dealing with this threat takes over. You start a fight or try harder to please or withdraw even further.

Awareness Activity

Make three lists with at least five items on each list. The headings are: "Five things I disliked about relating to my mother," "Five things I disliked about relating to my father" and "Five things I dislike about relating to my present partner." Notice the differences or similarities. With which parent is it easier to identify your dislikes? Is your relationship with your present partner more like the relationship you had with your mother or like the relationship you had with your father?

As a variation of this exercise, you might choose one of your siblings in place of a parent. Sometimes you are still working out unresolved sibling rivalry in your current relationships as well. It is not unusual for unresolved sibling rivalry issues to show up in current relationships. Your older brother or sister could have been given a parenting role and used it to drain off some of the hurt and anger they felt toward their parents. Frequently parents are glad to let the oldest child be a surrogate parent for the younger ones. This can force older children to grow up before they are ready and can lead to abusive acts of cruelty in the name of parenting.

SPECIFIC PATTERN 2a
Acting Weak and Helpless

This pattern is related to power and powerlessness. Most children feel powerless to change their situation, and when they grow up they try to use either one-down power by acting weak and helpless or one-up power by trying to dominate and control. The following awareness activity is designed to help you become aware of ways you utilize each of these co-dependent methods. Start with a clean sheet of paper and draw a line vertically down the center of the paper. On the left side of the page, write the heading: "Ways I Play Weak and Helpless Are . . ." and on the right side of the page, write the heading: "Ways I Dominate and Control Are . . ." After you have made your two lists, compare them and determine which you do better. Also notice how many could be placed on either list. The best one is being sick. In that way you can be weak and helpless *and* can control others to take care of you.

The way out of this co-dependent pattern is *through* it. Once you realize that in either case you are not getting what you really want, you may have to develop different strategies. The best way to get what you really want is to ask for it. The way to know when you have

51

broken this pattern is that you can ask for what you want in such a way that people are delighted to give it to you.

People will do almost anything to avoid asking for what they want. There is an overwhelming fear that someone will say "no" if we ask for what we want, and then we would have to deal with our feelings of being rejected. When you no longer have *resistance* to asking, people no longer have *resistance* to giving. What keeps people from giving you what you ask for even when they are capable of doing so is that they sense your uneasiness in asking and fear that you are trying to manipulate them or trick them in some way. Once you free yourself from the guilt or the resentment of "having to ask," then you will get what you want without having to resort to power plays.

Sometimes people get stuck in this pattern because they want to punish their parents by not growing up. They probably hope that by remaining a helpless child they can get their parents to take care of them. Unfortunately, it often works. A recent phenomenon has been thirty-year-old men and women still living at home and not growing up. They are often still being supported financially and emotionally by their parents, who often feel guilty for not raising more independent kids or who are afraid to let go and let their progeny grow up.

SPECIFIC PATTERN 2b
Life is a Struggle

Frequently people are addicted to struggle as a way of life. Since you are familiar with relationships where there is struggle, because of the struggles you had with your parents, you get very uncomfortable when your current relationships are going smoothly. It is too unfamiliar (un-family) for you and you have to create an upset in your current relationships.

Awareness Activity

The following awareness activity may help you better determine the effects of your earlier relationships on this pattern. Make a list of at least five things that your mother/father said or did to you as a child that you wish they hadn't said or done. As you look back at your childhood, you realize that these are the things that have affected you adversely in your adult relationships. (Example: "My father called me 'dumb' when I didn't understand something he said. Even to this day, I think I'm dumb if I don't understand something my partner says.")

This list represents some of the things that are likely to trigger an emotional response in you when you perceive someone close to you as behaving like one of your parents. These represent issues that are still unresolved. If they were resolved, they probably would not be listed by you. Look at each one and determine how that issue contributes to the struggles you may have in your current relationships.

One of the beliefs behind struggle as a way of life is that love has to be earned. This usually means that the harder you work to earn love from your spouse or loved one, the more you will appreciate their love when you finally earn it. Conversely, you may believe that if it comes easily without much work it cannot be worth very much. With this belief in the background, you could justifiably push away people who are easy to get along with and be drawn to those who are difficult to get along with. You will actually *attract* people who are hard to deal with.

While it is true that you can often learn much from a conflictual relationship, there is often an addictive and co-dependent quality to this behavior. It is perhaps a way of avoiding some deeper feelings or just a habitual and familiar way to be in a relationship. The avoidance part is often due to another belief that partners also need this struggle and, if you give up the struggle, they may no longer need you the way they did, and then they will surely leave you to find someone else to struggle with. In any kind of co-dependent relationship, this kind of fear can keep it going even though it looks from the outside that it is very destructive to both parties. Abusive and battering relationships would fall into this category. Also, the fear of abandonment or rejection often keeps these relationships going as do financial dependencies, usually on the part of the woman.

The fear of being left if you give up your dependencies is usually not born out in reality, but it is hard to convince dependent people to take the risk. What is true is that when a couple gets strong enough to change some of their mutual dependency patterns, the real love between them grows. I often tell clients and students the five magic words for successful relationships are "when need ends, love begins." People settle for relationships based upon co-dependency often because they do not have enough relationship skills to change the relationship into something better. When they learn these skills, such as negotiating skills or how to ask for what they want, they can move closer and improve their relationship.

ASKING FOR WHAT YOU WANT—The most important communication skill for breaking co-dependency is learning how to ask for what you want. As was mentioned in the previous section, people have strong emotional barriers to asking for what they want. In addition, many people simply lack the skills. I have used the following communication process successfully with many couples who were trying to break out of co-dependencies. It is helpful to get an agreement from the couple to be *willing* to ask for what they want one hundred percent of the time, even though it may never be necessary to ask all the time for everything. This kind of agreement can help a couple experiment with the skill and be aware of their own resistances. The steps in the process are as follows and can be initiated by either partner.

1. Make a request: "I would like you to give me a back rub."
2. Phrase it as a direct question ("Would you be willing to do that?") and then wait for an answer.
3. If the other says "yes," then proceed, but if the other person says "no" or hesitates, then you ask, "What are you willing to do?" (This is the negotiation phase.)
4. To negotiate further, you might ask: "Do you want anything in return from me if you agree to do this?"
5. This back and forth negotiation continues until there is an agreement ("Yes, I'll give you a back rub, but I would like a foot rub in return. Is that acceptable?"). This may seem rather cold and impersonal at first, but it works, and frequently it doesn't have to remain in such a structured form when couples learn how to use it to get their needs and wants met.

Very few couples who are locked into a co-dependent relationship use this kind of straight communication. The more people are willing to learn to ask and negotiate to get their needs and wants met, the less they need to try to manipulate and control to get their needs met in their relationships. Also, there is less struggle and co-dependency involved in the relationship.

SPECIFIC PATTERN 2c
Sexual Repression
This pattern is often very difficult for people to identify with because of the repression of sexual feelings in families. The pattern is that

your enjoyment of sex is limited by the degree to which you are still repressing your sexual feelings toward your parents. I hear statements from a member of a couple like, "I can't understand it. Since we got married she/he doesn't seem to want to have sex with me very much." Frequently, couples who live together do not have any trouble with their sexual expression toward each other until they get married. In other couples this pattern doesn't show up until the birth of the first child or even later.

The birth of a child places one partner in a mother's role and may then activate her husband's feelings toward his mother, who he now sees his wife being. Impotence can be the result, since the fear of sexual feelings increases as does the need to defend against them. Seeing his wife in a mother role can also activate other non-sexual feelings toward his mother that are then suddenly projected onto his wife. He may see her as controlling or rejecting or however he experienced himself in relationship with his mother while he was growing up. Often these are mutual patterns, because when he begins to project his unfinished business with his mother on his wife, his wife begins to see him as acting more like her father. The bedroom is a common place where these projections are acted out, since now there are at least four or six people sleeping in the same bed (his mother and father, and her mother and father, not to mention the two sets of grandparents for each).

Despite whatever sex education you may have received, your basic attitudes and beliefs regarding sex were learned from your parents, likely before you were ten years old. Even if they avoided any direct teaching, you learned by the sexual jokes that may have gotten told in your presence or by the way you saw your parents handle sexual issues with each other. In some families, sexual feelings are treated as healthy, normal feelings, while in other families they are regarded as bad, evil, dirty or not important. These distorted beliefs and attitudes certainly stay with you as you deal with sex in your adult relationships.

Awareness Activity

Although you may not have heard directly from each of your parents what their true feelings about sex were, you may now fantasize how they felt and probably be very accurate. In this activity, use a clean sheet of paper divided vertically into columns. The left-hand column should be titled: "If my mother told me her true thoughts and feelings about sex she would say . . ." The right-hand column should be titled: "If my father told me his true thoughts and feelings about sex he would say . . ." After you have listed five or more things under each, go back and look at each list, placing a check mark next to those thoughts and feelings that you identify within yourself. This will give you some clues as to how closely your thoughts and feelings about sex still mirror those of your parents.

Many men have sexual difficulties when their partner gets too eager or aggressive sexually. This can bring up repressed sexual feelings toward his mother. Some men cannot enjoy sex with their wives but enjoy it with a prostitute or with someone with whom they are not in a relationship. Other signs of this sexual repression in men and women often involve setting up triangles. A man or a woman may also be attracted to someone who is married, which recreates the competition they felt as children when they were trying to get affection or love from one of their parents without the other one being jealous.

I recall the following story told to me by a very creative four-year-old boy. I had asked him to make up a story about his family. He said, "Once there was a little boy and he loved his mommy and she loved him and when he got taller they got married and had lots of babies together and they were so happy." When I asked him about his father he said, "Oh, he got older and went away somewhere."

For most of us, daddy or mommy didn't go away somewhere, they stayed right there and denied and repressed their sexual feelings toward their children and sometimes toward each other. As I stated in Chapter 1, almost one in four women experiences sexual molestation before reaching the age of eighteen, with most of that occurring in their own family or with someone they knew. Much of the sexual abuse of children by family members is the result of denied and repressed sexual urges that are acted out inappropriately on those too young or too weak to defend against it.

Oddly, even more damage may result by repression of sexuality than by acting it out. While this is difficult to show in statistical ways, it is likely to be a factor in many of the teenage pregnancies. Many girls, when they move into puberty and develop breasts, find that for some unexplained reason their father will have nothing to do with them. Before becoming a woman, a girl may have received lots of physical affection from her father, only to have that removed from their relationship with no explanation. The connection that many teenagers make is that by becoming a woman, they have done something wrong or that being a woman is wrong. The truth is that their father could not deal with his sexual feelings toward his daughter so he withdrew. Rare is the father that can admit to these feelings. This also makes it unsafe for their daughters to learn how to flirt with a man in the usually safe confines of her home. Many young women have serious doubts about their femaleness as a result. Since these daughters often feel rejected as a woman by their fathers, they frequently seek reassurance from older teenaged men. This reassurance often involves sex and, frequently, an unplanned pregnancy results. The healthy response of a father with teenaged daughters would be for the father to tell them about his sexual feelings *and* to reassure them that he would not act on them, thus making physical contact safe and making other forms of reassurance unnecessary.

Also, the same phenomenon can occur with mothers and sons, leaving sons unsure of their manhood as well. I also recommend that mothers share any sexual feelings they have toward their sons and that both mothers and fathers help teens feel good about their growing and developing bodies. Maybe we will reach a level of trust in families where this kind of sharing of feelings and thoughts will be seen as normal and healthy. We do have a long way to go on this one.

We can only speculate on the adverse effects of repressed feelings on adult sexual relationships. We do know that frequently children are sexually abused by family members at an early age and are traumatized so much that they often repress the actual memory of this abuse until later in adulthood. Adult women and men in their thirties and forties are becoming aware of incest that happened during childhood. The panic and terror of being violated by a trusted parent can be among the most difficult family patterns to break. Contrary to popular stereotypes, incest affects all levels of the socioeconomic ladder and is as prevalent in educated families as it is in uneducated families. It knows no racial or religious boundaries and only on one fact is there strong agreement: The results are devastating to the child, leaving them with deep wounds, often severely crippling their sexual enjoyment later in life.

The Perfect Family

The story of Anne Marie illustrates this double standard.

I grew up in an upper middle-class family in a beautiful suburban neighborhood. We all went to church every Sunday and in every way we were the envy of all who knew us. The only problem is that we had an awful secret. I was the youngest child of seven, and I guess when I was born my parents decided not to have any more children. Being good Catholics for whom birth control was a mortal sin, the only alternative for my parents was abstinence. I didn't know this then, but apparently my father decided to get even with my mother for not having sex with him by forcing his attention on my older sisters. I can only remember back to about age eight when it began with me, although I could have been even younger. I can remember hearing my parents' door open every morning before I got up, and I could hear my father's foot-steps as he came down the hall. He would come into my room and crawl in bed with me. I can remember him rubbing his erect penis up against me and I can remember his hands on my genitals, but then I blank out. I don't remember what happened after that. I would just freeze with terror and everything would go blank.

This happened every morning of my life from the time I was eight years old until I left for college. It was the same every day. I was absolutely terrified around my father and tried to do every-thing I could to avoid contact with him during the day or in the evening. The feelings of terror would start when I heard his car drive up the driveway. My mother was always chiding me for not being nicer to my father. She would tell me how I had hurt his feelings by not paying enough attention to him.

After I left home I forgot about that all happening. In fact, later it seemed like just a bad dream. After college I married a man they approved of and our first couple of years were rough sexually, but I never connected any of our difficulties to my father. I guess I had really married someone more like my mother, whom I got along with but never felt close to. It wasn't until my early forties that any memory of what happened with my father began to return. After a messy divorce from Bob, mostly brought about by my desire to become my own person, I began to have trouble being sexually responsive to men. I hadn't had much experience sexually, so at first I thought it was just my lack of experience. However, my lack of sexual responsiveness got worse with experience.

Finally, I dated and eventually married a man who helped bring it all to the surface. I wanted so much to be able to enjoy sex with him but I couldn't. Every time we made love I could feel

the panic and terror rise in me, and then I would just freeze. I
tried everything I knew, including hypnosis and therapy, but with
few results. There were lots of things that my husband said or did
that would remind me of my father, and I could feel my body
stiffen each time one of those things would happen. I felt this
dark mass over my left shoulder and it was always present. I
never seemed to escape it but, if I was careful, I could keep it
from taking over under most conditions, but sexually it was real
difficult to avoid. It seemed as if one small thing that my husband
did, the way he looked at me or if he did something I hadn't anticipated, and I would be flooded by the old feelings, and the pain
in my body would be almost too much to bear.

My husband was understanding, but he, too, began losing
patience with me. Eventually I decided to confront my father by
writing him a letter, only to have him go senile as a result. My
mother apparently knew a lot about what was going on and only
once was I able to talk to her. All she could say was 'I was too
afraid of him to do anything to stop him.' I felt so guilty and
ashamed that *I* wasn't able to do anything to stop him. I often
thought, 'Why me? Why does he have to pick on me? What have
I done to deserve this?'

Lately, I have been despairing about all this. I wish I had
started work on all this earlier in my life. I waited over thirty-five
years before I even knew what was causing me these problems.
That is too long to bury something as pervasive as this. I told my
husband that I don't think I will ever be free of these problems
and that I'm not sure I want to go on living. He tried to offer me
some hope but he, too, is getting worried that we can't get
through this.

A week after Anne Marie told me all this, she was killed in an accident. After her death, one of her four older sister revealed that she,
too, was a victim of her father's lust but was older when it happened
and was able to fight him off. This sister also found out that the other
three sisters were incest victims as well, although they banded together to protect themselves from their father. It did not occur to any
of them that Anne Marie might have suffered the same fate. The con-
spiracy of silence prevented Anne Marie from knowing that she was
not alone in her plight. She truly believed that there was something
wrong with her and that the others were spared because whatever was
wrong with her was not wrong with them.

CHAPTER SIX

Living Out Your Parents' Relationship

*I cannot give you the formula for
success, but I can give you the
formula for failure—which is to
try to please everybody.*
—HERBERT BAYARD SWOPE

Dealing With Your Parents' Relationship

Your training in how to have a relationship came mainly
from observing your parents' relationship or the relationship of those
people who were most often in a parenting role. You spent literally
thousands of hours observing your parents in relationship with each
other. Much of this training was not at a conscious level, and the patterns of relationship that you learned were certainly not conscious to
you. Do you remember after finding out about sex, trying to imagine
your parents having sex together? Much of what they did in their relationship and why they did it probably remains a mystery to you.
However, what you learned unconsciously forms a template, a program, for how to have a relationship.

Many children vow that when they become adults they are going
to have a better, or at least different, relationship from that of their
parents' relationship, only to find themselves recreating the same kind
of relationship that their parents had. What happens is that this unconscious program directs your behavior in situations that are familiar
(family) to you and remind you of your family of origin. You shouldn't
be surprised to find this out about yourself, because a natural, normal

way that people learn is by modeling or copying the behavior of others in order to learn it for themselves.

Even though you may consciously desire to move away from that program or change it, until you bring the program into conscious awareness, you cannot change the program or be free from it. Part of the problem is that at a more basic level, you haven't emotionally or psychologically separated from your parents. Very few children are given the support and tools to become emotionally independent of their parents by the time they are adults. Also, very few parents know how to give that support or teach the necessary independence tools to their children. Even people who rebel and think they have broken free are still emotionally tied to the energy patterns of their family.

Since you are likely still tied to the energy patterns of your parents, they may still be able to have you live out the unfulfilled parts of their relationship. The message was often given very directly in the advice they gave us: "Get an education, so you won't have to struggle so hard like we had to." Or, "Don't get married so soon; see the world first." However, these messages may be paired with other messages that say the opposite, such as, "Be careful; don't take too many risks," or even more covert messages that indicate they would be envious or jealous if you were more successful at your relationships than they were. Mostly this is due to their unhealed narcissistic wounds which prevent them from supporting their children's efforts to have better relationships, jobs, houses, etc.

I had a recent illustration of this principle at work. We had our house for sale because of a desire to move to a smaller house. A young couple with a growing family came to look at the house and they loved it. The price did not seem to be an issue, and we could tell they really wanted the house. They went from room to room talking very excitedly about where they would put this or that piece of furniture.

Several days later they returned with the husband's parents who were visiting from out of town. As the parents walked through the house with their son and daughter-in-law, they could not find anything they liked about the house. They said it was too big and pretentious for them. I could see the excitement for the house being drained out of this young couple by his parents' attitude, especially the attitude of his father. I asked the husband's father what kind of house he and his wife lived in and found out that it was a much smaller house, even though it cost about as much as our house was selling for. Instead of seeing this as a possible bargain for their son, they seemed to resent the fact that their son would want to have a larger and more "showy" house than they had. I don't know what additional pressures they put on their son and daughter-in-law, but the young couple called back the next day to tell us that they were going to look for a smaller house.

You may feel guilty (fear of punishment) when you achieve something on your own that is beyond the level of what your parents achieved. Getting a good paying job, an advanced degree, a nice house, etc. can activate a fear in you that your parents may not approve or may feel bad that they couldn't achieve this. Often these feelings and thoughts are difficult to identify, and you may even dismiss them as unimportant. They are signals or clues that tell you that some unspoken rule or expectation may have been broken.

Loyalty and Legacy Issues

These two issues form a context for helping you understand why it is so hard to break your family patterns and why you tend to repeat self-defeating and destructive behavior patterns in the next generation. Laing (1965) and Stierlin (1976) both describe the process by which parents are able to exact an undying loyalty from their children. First, it usually begins very early in life, before children have any idea what is being done. Certainly the church, the schools and the society in general do nothing to counter the blind acceptance of filial loyalty supported by expressions like "Honor thy father and mother" and "Blood runs thicker than water."

Actually, you don't realize until much later what a debt you may have assumed toward your parents. For many people, the debt may seem endless and may require you to put this debt before any other human commitment. No matter how abusive or damaging your relationship with your parents was for you, you may still feel obligated to pay that debt in full, even if it totally depletes you of all your resources.

Because of your debts of undying loyalty, supposedly you can enjoy the legacy of being part of a family. We all were born into a family, and by the accident of birth we inherited the family legacy and the family name. This also means that whatever happens to you as a result of growing up in your family has to be regarded as part of your legacy. This provides you with a kind of deterministic view of your family of origin and requires you to accept your curse of fate as graciously or loyally as possible.

When you put the loyalty debt and the legacy curse together, you have an unbeatable combination. This is why it is so difficult to let go of your parents' relationship and why you are so obsessed with trying to make it better or to fix it for them. You may see this as a legitimate way to repay the debts you owe. You can easily get very frustrated and scared when your parents refuse your offers of help. This may bring up fears in you that your indebtedness will never end and that they control how the debt is to be repaid (as long as your parents are still alive). This fear is not entirely unfounded, and many parents do use this debt of loyalty and curse of legacy to manipulate and control their children.

When you grow up, these loyalty and legacy issues remain to confuse you in your dealings with your own family. You may want to be a better parent to your own children but feel somehow disloyal if you treat your children better than the way your parents treated you. Also, this allows you to deny any guilt you might have over treating your children poorly, because you can justify your behavior by believing that you are doing it out of a sense of loyalty to your parents.

It is important that you find effective ways to take care of this debt of loyalty and legacy; otherwise, you can become stagnated in your family patterns. This is often the most difficult general pattern of all to break through. Because it is so basic to the intergenerational foundation of a family, it may be the last one to become conscious. No one escapes without having to deal with the issues of loyalty and legacy. In healthy families, these issues are handled in more matter-of-fact ways, and family members are not encumbered by excessive filial loyalties and legacy issues.

However, in families where parents have strong narcissistic attachments to their children, these issues can be very sticky indeed. One such example of this came to my attention recently. Many years ago, a mother and daughter had opened a gift shop together in the family home. They closed in the front porch and converted the living room into a gift shop. The arrangement worked well, but the mother complained for many years about having to give up her living room for her business. When she retired, the shop was closed and the living room was restored to its original use, much to her delight. She said, "I finally got my living room back again."

It was about that time that her daughter decided to open up a gift shop in her own home and decided against using her living room, planning instead to add a shop on the back of her house. When her mother heard about this plan, she became very upset and protested, "You can't do that. You have to use your living room for the shop the way I had to do." The daughter, without realizing it, had committed a disloyal act by wanting to avoid a problem that she had heard her mother complain about for years. The daughter was astonished at how angry and blatant her mother was and also began to wonder about other less obvious ways she was being asked to be loyal to her parents.

In this next example, these loyalty and legacy issues crossed three generations. A grandfather broke with his family pattern by leaving the farm and going to work for a company in the city. His son then stayed in the city, but started his own business. Now the grandson was caught in a situation of conflicting loyalties in which he wasn't sure whether to work for others or go in business for himself. As a result, he spent his life futilely fighting for collective causes while always second-guessing his career choice, no matter how successful he was. Finally he found an effective way to blend these two seemingly conflicting legacies by receiving recognition for his individual effort on behalf of a collective cause. The loyalty debt was repaid effectively.

In cases of separation, death or divorce, there is the issue of split loyalties, although this also can occur in families where one parent tries to use the children against the other parent. If children are pulled into taking sides, parents can create impossible double-bind situations for them to deal with. Overt examples of this are when one parent complains to the children about the things that are wrong with the other parent. Or the children may be put in the middle of fights between the parents. I know of some families where the children are asked to be the messengers: "Go tell your father I said he is a jerk." Sometimes children will develop problems in hopes of getting the parents to resolve their conflicts. One anorexic girl had a dream where she saw her parents dying and lying next to adjoining grave sites. She realized that if she chose to feed one of them, the other would die. She couldn't choose which one to take care of.

These kinds of divided loyalties get even worse in situations such as those in which a mother and her parents are aligned against the father. The child is expected to join with his mother and grandparents against his father. The child may feel totally immobilized and not know how to balance these loyalties. If these loyalty issues are not balanced, they can later lead to a crippling ambivalence toward one's own spouse and children. The situation will replay itself in some way, constellating an unresolved issue of divided loyalties.

Awareness Activity

As a way to begin to identify your own loyalty debt and legacy curse, complete the following awareness activity. Make a list of the debts you believe you owe your parents. ("Take care of them if they are sick", "Have grandchildren for them", "Be successful for them.") Also list the ways you have tried to repay the debt you believe you owe. ("Buy them nice gifts at Christmas and birthdays", "Give them a grandson to carry on the family name.") Finally, list the things that you believe you cannot say or do because of your loyalty to them.

After you have made your list, you also may want to discuss the list with your spouse. He or she also has a set of loyalty and legacy issues, and it is good to compare what they are and how you can support each other in dealing with these issues.

I am also reminded of an example of a family who had lots of secrets and covert activities because the matriarch of the family was very religious and did not approve of drinking alcohol or smoking cigarettes or of any profanities even said in jokes. When this matriarch came to visit her children, all the ash trays were removed, the liquor was hidden up in the closet and everyone was careful about using any profanity.

One child, however, was spared all this control. When he went away to college, he escaped all these loyalty and legacy issues. When he came home from college at vacation time, he would enter his mother's house with a quart of whisky under one arm, a cigarette hanging out of his mouth and cursing a blue streak. While everyone was shocked that he could get away with this, his mother never said anything to him, except that she prayed extra in church for him last Sunday. After he returned to college, he would be the subject of long discussions among the other siblings who just couldn't figure out how he could get away with being so disloyal. They also envied him but were always too scared to risk doing what he had done.

SPECIFIC PATTERN 3a
The Parentized Child

When we were children, it was in our best interest to have good parents and a stable family. These important elements in your life formed the foundation for your earliest development. The role of parents and family is to provide the support and nurturing necessary for you to develop into fully independent, separate human beings. However, narcissistically deprived parents *could not* and *did not* provide the necessary support and nurturing for you to develop emotional and psychological separateness. Instead, you were raised to become objects who will focus all your attention on your parents, take what they say and do seriously, respect them and follow them around. (Exactly what you wished your parents had provided for you.)

As a newborn baby, you were completely dependent on your parents and you did everything you could to preserve the bond you had with them. Given that kind of situation, parents can do almost anything to you: they can beat you, teach you good and bad habits, mold you and punish you without any repercussions for them. You were too young to defend yourself from these influences, so the consequences of these actions remain buried in your psyche. Because they were done to you so early in life, you were not aware of what was done to you, what was taken from you, what you were losing in the process and who you really were. If this was done from the very beginning of life, you would not have a will of your own; your only existence would be to function as an extension of the will of your parents. One woman expressed it as follows: "I was *their* child. I did what they told me to. I wasn't separate from them. I wasn't a person."

Your legacy from being raised in a family where you were not allowed to develop a separate will of your own is that you become "parentized." That is, your sole function becomes one of service to your parents. You are asked to put aside any of your needs and personal strivings and instead pay close attention to the wants, needs and personal strivings of your parents. In this situation, you would do almost anything to preserve the well-being of your parents and your family. If the family looks like it is going to break up, you may sacrifice yourself to save the family. You may fail in school, shoplift, take drugs, become anorexic, attempt suicide or do something that you believe will divert attention away from the problems your parents have.

66

You often become the identified patient in family therapy, thus hoping to get your parents to work on their problems.

One thing is sure—unless the pattern is broken, you who have been parentized will not be able to give freely to your own spouse or children. The loyalty you were taught to have to even excessive demands and expectations of your parents can make it impossible for you to form a deep commitment to your spouse or intimates and leads to a stiffening or freezing of your inner life. Your only choice is to live what Jung called "the unauthentic life," a life without inner conviction or direction.

Rebels do not escape this tyranny either. Sometimes a couple will share their denial of strong loyalty ties to their family of origin. Instead, the rebel remains tied to the loyalty system in his or her posture of opposition. A disloyal rebel can also function to preserve the family by getting them to mobilize against him or her.

In some family systems, if one sibling achieves much success, another sibling manifests failure, which keeps the system in balance. In the same way, one child can get "hooded" into taking care of his/her parents because of the transgressions of another sibling. The conforming child can look good in this system and become a good boy or a nice girl. One "nice girl" said, "They told me who I was. I didn't realize until I was thirty-five years old that I was not part of them."

Since this "parentizing" condition is so damaging to your attempts to form intimate, effective adult relationships, it is necessary to first achieve some degree of separation or emancipation from the domination and control of your parents' will. Fortunately, even though you may have been subjected to severe punishment to make you obey, it is usually impossible to totally break a person's free will. Certainly you were crippled emotionally because of your experiences, but there remains enough of a separate will in most of you, except in some severely psychotic people, which you can use to begin to build a separate identity.

Awareness Activity

In this activity, make a list of the ways your parents supported and promoted your dependency on them. Then make another list of the ways your parents supported and promoted your independence from them. These lists may help you begin to be aware of how this process operated in your family. One client put it this way: "They wanted me to be very feminine, but being feminine meant being weak, fragile and dependent. When I wasn't being one or all of these ways, I was accused of being unfeminine. Being independent was never encouraged because that was being unfeminine." Another client said, "The main value I remember being taught was how important it was to be a good boy—which meant that I was always supposed to do as I was told and not question it. I remember that this was so important to my parents and grandparents that they gave me money if I got A's in deportment in school [now called citizenship or conduct], not math or reading, but deportment."

Parentized children are taught to value those things that make it easier for their parents to manipulate and control them. So often we are taught these values by parents and teachers who acted as if they were teaching us these things for our own good. The following are examples of beliefs that are often taught this way.

1. Parents always deserve respect no matter what they say or do.
2. Children never deserve respect no matter what they say or do.
3. Too much self-esteem is not good. Humility is always the best policy.
4. Only bad people get angry.
5. Always put the needs of parents and others ahead of your own needs.
6. You learn to get along in the world by obeying rules without question.
7. Tenderness is a sign of weakness. People will take advantage of you if you show tenderness.
8. Learning to deal with unfairness and coldness is good preparation for life.
9. You have to behave the way others want you to behave in order to get along.
10. Parents and adults are always right. They are never wrong no matter what they say or do.
11. Your body is something smelly and dirty and should be hidden from others.
12. Any strong feelings should be avoided because they are harmful.

13. Being loyal to one's parents' and family's ways is very honorable.

14. Be careful not to do anything that would damage the family name, reputation, etc.

You might identify with some of these ideals and values as ones that you were taught, or add some of your own. You might think about these now, asking yourself honestly if these were taught to you for your own good or for the good of your parents and others who wanted to control you.

These were the values and ideals that were taught in German families prior to the rise of Hitler. Hitler merely took these ideals a step further. Rudolf Hess, one of Hitler's top propagandists, stated this clearly in his speech of June 30, 1934: "We note with pride that one man remains beyond all criticism, and that is the Furhrer (Father). This is because everyone senses and knows: he is always right, and he will always be right. The National Socialism of all of us is anchored in uncritical loyalty, in a surrender to the Furhrer that does not ask about the why in individual cases, in the silent execution of his orders."

Biographies of all the leading figures in the Third Reich showed that they were all parentized children with strict and rigid upbringing. Their loyalty to the Furhrer and the ideals of the Father allowed them to justify murdering over one million Jewish children, thus enabling them to release the hatred they felt at the way their own child qualities were stifled. In addition, while they were murdering Jewish children, they were also murdering the child within themselves as obedient loyal servants.

CHAPTER SEVEN

Breaking the Bonds of Loyalty and Legacy

We forfeit three-fourths of ourselves in order to be like other people.
—ARTHUR SCHOPENHAUER

Breaking free from these bonds of loyalty and legacy can be frightening, indeed, and this chapter will explore ways to begin that process as you move to the other two specific patterns: "The Fear of Success" and "Crossing the Threshold."

SPECIFIC PATTERN 3b
The Fear of Success

There are several aspects to the fear of success. One of them is a fear of punishment (guilt) if you are more successful than your parents were. This is related to your debt of loyalty and the legacy curse discussed earlier. Certainly, if you were not encouraged to be independent of your parents, any efforts in that direction could be seen by them as evidence of your disloyalty.

To counter this kind of oppression through guilt, you may have to develop some weapons of your own, one of which may be to fail and not live up to parental expectations, thus punishing your parents and trying to get them to feel guilty enough to give up their expectations. This rarely works and also leads to more pain and suffering for the child who fails. It is more of a lose-lose strategy for getting even, but no growth usually results from this approach.

70

Another related approach may also yield similar results. This involves a fear of actually being successful and getting everything you want. Generally what keeps you from getting what you want is your old anger at being treated unfairly by your parents. You can use that as a reason for not being successful, so if you get what it is you want *you may have to give up your old anger toward your parents.* Another fear is that as your anger dissipates, it may open up feelings of sadness, hurt and pain from your childhood. We may actually fear these feelings, so it is easier not to be too successful rather than risk an encounter with these unknown feelings. The fear may be that the feelings will overwhelm you or that you might go crazy or disintegrate if you had to re-experience these feelings.

Awareness Activity

One way to bring to awareness your fears of success is through the following activity. We all have "edges," or boundaries, about how successful we can be or the places we believe we cannot go beyond without some superhuman effort or without something bad happening. These "edges" were likely programmed into us during childhood, and they often go unchallenged into adult life. In each of the categories listed below, indicate what it is you can't do. For example, in sports I might say, "I can't be an 'A' tennis player." The categories for this list are "Relationships", "Career", "Parenting", "Family", "My Body", "Sports", "My Feelings", "Talents", "Hobbies", "Money", "Religion", "Travel", "Health", "Leisure Time", "Friends" and "My House." You can add any others of your own choosing.

Under each category, write the words "I can't . . ." and then complete the sentence. If you go blank and can't think of an edge, keep writing "I can't" until you think of something to write. Write everything you think of, even if it seems silly, stupid or not true. When you finish this part of the activity, go back over what you have written and try to identify where the "I can't" might have originated. See if you can determine whether or not you were told *not* to do this by one of your parents. Frequently you take on the fears of your parents as your own. By becoming aware of the fears you took on from others, you are then in a better position to give back (for-give) these fears to their rightful owner.

SPECIFIC PATTERN 3c
Crossing the Threshold

The most common pattern that holds you back is a fear of the unknown. In relationships, your ability to take the risks to change and grow may be limited by the kind of modeling of this you received from observing your parents' relationship. If you saw your parents taking risks to grow and change, you might be more willing to do the same in your relationships. If you saw your parents shy away from growth and change by trying to avoid conflict or by not living their own dreams and ideals, you may feel a need to live out your parents' dreams but also you may feel a lack of skills. In addition, another strong force calls you from within. We all want to be able to live an authentic life where we feel we are directing the major aspects of our own life. This desire for independence is a basic human need and has been a major striving of humankind throughout history.

Joseph Campbell (1968), one of the world's leading authorities on mythology, found the keys of this journey embedded in the myths and fairy tales of all cultures. Myths and fairy tales were not stories used to entertain children; they were teaching stories for adults to help them learn the process of growth and change. Campbell calls the process the *hero's journey* or the *journey of transformation*. The major steps in the process are:

1. The Call to Awaken
2. Refusing the Call
3. The False Call
4. Answering the Call
5. Gathering Allies
6. Crossing the Threshold
7. The Road of Trials
8. The Sacred Marriage
9. The Apotheosis
10. The Return
11. The Master of Both Worlds

The diagram he uses shows that it is a circular journey and it could take a lifetime to complete. Some people cycle through it many times during their lifetime, while others hardly ever get started. I will describe each step, showing how it might occur in your life. (Chapter 21 contains a description of my own journey of transformation.)

The Call to Awaken usually comes from an external event or inner awareness that causes you to stop and think about your life and where you are going. It often is an opportunity to change or it can be a block to what you have been doing. It may be caused by an illness, getting fired, being offered a new job, moving to a new location, being inspired by a book, movie or play, the betrayal of a friend, losing a loved one or the breaking up of a love relationship—all these can be calls to you to awaken or to take a closer look at your life and change directions.

You may *Refuse the Call* by telling yourself that it isn't the right time or by finding some reason why you cannot answer this call. If you refuse the call, it will come again, perhaps ringing louder in some way to get your attention. Some people spend a lifetime stuck in this part of the process: receiving a call to awaken and then refusing the call and going back to business as usual. Fear of the unknown and a feeling of not being prepared can keep you from answering the call.

Sometimes you may answer *A False Call* when you agree to do something for someone else but ignore your own callings. Old loyalty debts can make you feel as though you have to do this for others before you can really do what you want to do. You can chair a committee, run for public office, work on a project with others or take a job you don't want, thinking you are answering the call, only to realize later that you avoided your own callings.

Answering the Call usually involves some risk, trying something new or waking up to your own inertia or family patterns. It involves a conscious decision to move ahead, to challenge yourself to new growth and awareness. At first we may not even know how we are going to do this, but gradually the way emerges as we *Gather Allies* to help us. The word "ally" comes from a Greek word that means "silly," so our allies may appear silly to us at first. They may find us, rather than our having to search for them. Books may fall off the shelves into our hands in bookstores, someone may give us a book to read or we may have a chance meeting with an interesting stranger. We find that allies show up in unexpected places. An ally is some information, support or person with permission that tells us we are on the right track and helps us learn how to stay more awake.

When we feel we have gathered enough allies, we finally face a decision to *Cross the Threshold*. This is the point to which we have prepared ourselves as much as we can and still realize that we must leap into the unknown. The crossing of the threshold really represents a leap of faith, and usually there are a number of fears to overcome, each representing an inner threshold with which to deal. First there is the *silliness threshold* that involves the fear of appearing foolish to others. It may bring up loyalty and legacy issues about what members of our family can and can't do. The *sanity threshold* is a fear that a leap into the unknown will cause us to go crazy because we will be out of control or unable to control what happens. The *knowledge threshold* can be a fear of finding out something that invalidates your way of thinking about the world. A *trust threshold* reflects our vulnerability and a fear of being hurt. We also may experience a *love threshold* where we fear that we will lose the love of our loved ones if we cross the threshold. Finally, a *survival threshold* may loom up in front of us with a fear of death or abandonment resulting from crossing the threshold.

If you decide to cross the threshold, you are faced with the *Road of Trials*. These tests of courage usually require that your lessons have been learned well. They usually occur in such a way that you cannot go back and study your notes or think it over for a while. You have to act in new ways, but you find that you have internalized the information and resources necessary to meet the tests.

During the road of trials, you may be forced to endure the *dark night of the soul* when the bottom may drop out of your world. This could involve the death of a loved one, the ending of a career, a serious illness or an accident that in some way tests you beyond anything you have ever experienced. You usually pull out of this experience being much stronger and more integrated, leading you to the next step which is the *Sacred Marriage*. This is the time when you take back your projections and experience a sense of inner unity between your developed and previously projected parts. It is like a marriage of your masculine and feminine sides. This is usually the time where you are consciously aware enough of yourself and your various parts that you can own your parts instead of projecting them on others.

Also about the same time, you may experience an *Apotheosis,* which is a merger of your higher self and your lower self. This may be when you begin to recognize your true self and your false self and begin to bring the two together in a more integrated way. You may also have dealt with your anger and sorrow enough to reach a place of compassion for yourself and your parents. It is a time of inner healing.

The journey may seem complete at this stage, but it is only half

74

finished. Now you must take all this new knowledge and *Return* to consciousness and learn to live it in your everyday world. This is not an easy task, for the everyday world contains all the traps and family patterns that may entice you to go back to sleep again. There are prices to pay for gaining access to the depths. Your friends and loved ones may not understand, you may be tested and criticized by peers. You also may find that the common, ordinary, banal world no longer holds any appeal for you, and you may wish to return to the safety of your rich inner world. To put it simply, it becomes damn difficult to live in the world you were used to. You must learn to bring the knowledge from your depths into your everyday world and learn how to integrate the two worlds. This also involves a threshold to cross with many of the same fears to face that you faced upon entering the underworld. You may fear that people will think you are silly because you take an hour a day to meditate, or write in your journal or what-ever daily practices you use. You also fear that the split you feel be-tween the inner and outer worlds will drive you crazy. This step involves learning to overcome these and the other threshold fears as well as learning to become *Master of Both Worlds*. This means that you can live in the ordinary, everyday world and still enjoy your deep connections, in fact bringing them into your conscious awareness dur-ing your daily routines and rituals.

The following Zen koan illustrates this last phase of the journey:

> Before I was transformed, the snows of Mt. Fuji were just the snows of Mt. Fuji and the waters of the Tassajara were just the waters of the Tassajara. While I was on the journey of transfor-mation, the snows of Mt. Fuji were no longer just the snows of Mt. Fuji and the waters of the Tassajara were no longer just the waters of the Tassajara. After I was transformed, the snows of Mt. Fuji were just the snows of Mt. Fuji and the waters of the Tassajara were just the waters of the Tassajara.

Awareness Activity

In order to personalize this journey, go back and look at each step in terms of where you see yourself at present in the process and what events and activities of your life fit with the various steps in the pro-cess. This activity may help you gain a broader perspective on your life and support you to go forward with at least a road map to help guide your journey.

75

CHAPTER EIGHT

It's for Your Own Good

> *The further backward you can look,*
> *the further backward you are likely*
> *to see.*
>
> —WINSTON CHURCHILL

In the previous chapters you have learned that much of the damage to your psyche was done before you were developmentally able to understand what was being done and why it was being done. Even worse, because you don't remember what happened, you are very likely to have a compulsion to repeat what was done to you with your own children and believe you are doing it for their own good. Locked within you are many secrets and misperceptions. To break the vicious cycle of cruelty, first you have to uncover your deepest feelings and find an appropriate way to express them as fully as possible.

The process of uncovering these forgotten feelings requires you to become more conscious of the problems in your current relationships that provide you with clues to childhood and family of origin issues. In addition, the process of uncovering these feelings often requires a better knowledge of what usually happens in the early development of a child and what feelings might likely result from these events of early childhood. This chapter will present an overview of the themes and stages of early development with a particular emphasis on the process of completing our second or psychological birth. This is where your forgotten feelings often reside.

The Course of Early Development

Because the birth process itself is so important in your development, we will deal with it separately in Chapter 11. The most critical process in the first two to three years following your physical birth is the gradual movement from co-dependence to independence where you finally achieve, if you are lucky, your second or psychological birth. This process was first described by Sigmund Freud, but he lacked a full understanding of the process. In the past twenty-five years, through the brilliant research of Dr. Margaret Mahler, we have developed a rather complete picture of this vital life process. We now know enough about the process to know what is necessary to shepherd an infant through this process, and we know what happens to people in adult life when they get stuck in certain stages of the process.

The single most important, driving, developmental task of infants before the age of three is to complete what nature has left incomplete and achieve their psychological birth, giving them selfhood and an identity separate from their mother. The degree to which infants are able to complete this process on schedule in those crucial three years will determine to a large degree the amount of selfhood and separate identify they will have for the rest of their lives. Development is a continuous process from conception to death, and anything not completed on schedule will have to be dragged along as excess baggage until another "slow down" or rest period in development makes it possible for those issues to recycle again to get completed.

Hardly anyone survives childhood without some handicap or developmental problem due to the incompleteness of a developmental task. Some of these handicaps are never overcome. They remain with you for the rest of your life as you adapt to them and learn to live a more limited life. Still others work around these severe handicaps and become healthy, happy adults. Some less fortunate people become psychotic or suffer from debilitating disorders such as drug and/or alcohol addiction.

Margaret Mahler (1967) was the first to use the term "symbiosis" to describe the normal relationship between mother and a newborn child. In this relationship, which is necessary for the survival of the child, a state of biological co-dependency develops between mother and child. One cannot exist fully without the other. The baby cries and the mother lactates.

77

In this state of oneness, the infant is filled with the bliss of un-conditional love and often radiates this love out to the mother. This is the basic condition for all human love. However, sometimes an illness to the mother or child following the physical birth can interfere with the development of oneness or complete bonding that both mother and child feel. The responsibility of being a mother and having to care for a helpless creature creates much anxiety or depression for many mothers, which an infant intuitively feels while being fed or held or having diapers changed.

Around the age of two, another form of human love begins to emerge as the infant begins to separate from this state of co-dependency with his or her mother and learns to love freedom or sep-arateness. If this is not completed on schedule, all later human rela-tionships become the staging ground for your attempts to reconcile these seemingly conflicting longings for co-dependency and independ-ence. The process of reconciliation of these conflicting issues is called the development of object constancy. Object constancy is the process of being able to hold yourself and others as a more or less constant object, seeing each with good and bad qualities. People with weak ob-ject constancy are easily crushed by a critical remark by someone else, or they tend to see themselves, the world and other people as all good or all bad. They tend to split their objects along some predeter-mined criterion of good and bad. They are able to feel co-dependency or independence without being able to integrate both of these aspects in a relationship. They are either totally dependent or they become aloof and act counter-dependent or separate.

If the process for developing oneness and the process for devel-oping separateness both go according to nature's plan, then you will be able to fully enjoy both oneness and separateness aided by strong ob-ject constancy in your adult relationships. The problems you encounter in adult relationships with oneness, separateness or object constancy require you to go back to early childhood to look at these three inter-related processes and to discover what might have gone wrong.

Limbo

The period from birth to about six weeks is described as the period of limbo for the infant. The old environment of the womb is gone and the new environment of psychological oneness has yet to form. A sense of biological symbiosis is present almost immediately after birth, but it takes about six weeks for the two people to get to know each other and develop a psychological relationship of oneness.

The foundation for self-esteem of the child is imbedded in these first weeks of contact. Every child has a legitimate narcissistic need to be seen, understood, taken seriously and respected by his or her mother. One of the ways this gets communicated during the early stage of development is through the mother's ability to be a mirror for the child. While being held or fed, the child gazes up at his/her mother's face and sees him/herself mirrored there. Infants learn who they are in this manner. If the mother is unable to mirror the child because of her own fears, expectations and plans for the child, then the child would not see him/herself in his/her mother's face and would miss a vital step in the development of selfhood. Mothers must be able to put aside their own needs and allow themselves to be used by their children. Children who are mirrored during this stage will be able to develop a healthy narcissism, which is essential for the later stages of ego development.

Alice Miller (1981) lists the following ways in which parents can foster the development of healthy narcissism in children. As you read this list ask yourself, "Can I imagine my parents doing these things for me when I was a child?"

• Reacting calmly and reassuringly to your aggressive impulses.
• Supporting your attempts to become separate and autonomous instead of seeing them as an attack or threat.
• Allowing you to experience and express your ordinary impulses such as rage, jealousy or defiance.
• Not requiring that you please them with your behavior so you can develop and exhibit whatever is active in you during each developmental stage.
• Allowing you to use them by being at your disposal when you need them.
• Permitting you to express conflicting or ambivalent feelings and taking those seriously.
• Seeing you as separate from them, as someone with his or her own needs, wishes, fears, dreams and accomplishments.

Often the mother's first impression of the infant can color the way her psychological relationship with the child develops. At first, some mothers don't believe that the baby is theirs. They have carried fantasies, fears, hopes and dreams about this child during their pregnancy that greatly influence their first impression. Mothers are often afraid of their newborn or they are joyful. Often stories told about your birth and your mother's first impressions can help you understand what the quality of your psychological relationship was. Carol's story illustrates this.

Original Guilt

Carol was in her early thirties when she first came to see me. Outwardly she had been very successful in her life. She was married to a handsome, seemingly loving man, had three beautiful children and had been a successful teacher and community leader. Inside, however, Carol felt empty and not lovable. She had lots of trouble getting along with her mother whom she saw as controlling her. After several sessions together, mostly gathering background information, I asked her what the story of her birth was. She said that she had a difficult birth and her mother had had complications. Then she said, "The story I heard over and over was that my mother was a very beautiful woman, and after she had me her figure changed and she gained weight and never lost the weight. It was like I had caused her to lose her beauty. This is why I always feel so guilty around her. She calls me up and complains about her life and is always making cutting remarks about my successes." Carol went on to realize that her lack of enjoyment of life was all related to the guilt she had about what happened to her mother during childbirth. With support from me, she was able to talk to her mother about this problem. As a result of confronting her mother, she began to build a better relationship with her in which she felt free to express her feelings and not be controlled by her mother's problems.

Although it seems that infants are powerless over the elements of their environment, they do come into the world equipped with these helpful qualities: 1) they can shut out disturbing sights and sounds, 2) they can appear helpless and 3) they have a smiling reflex. These three innate mechanisms make it possible for the child to 1) protect its delicate nervous system, 2) get picked up and have its needs tended to and 3) elicit pleasant responses from others.

Oneness

During the period of time from about six weeks to five months, the infant develops total dependence on its mother. There is no outside

80

environment for the child without a mother. Two common orienting movements of the infant at this age are molding and stiffening. Molding refers to an inner-directedness and a melting of the boundaries between mother and child. It involves fetal-like movements. Stiffening refers to the outer-directed behaviors of looking, listening, reaching and grasping, and thrusting outward with arms and legs.

Separateness Begins

At about five months, the first visible stirrings of separateness occur. By five months the baby is somewhat aware of his or her body boundaries, but still only vaguely. This can be a confusing time for both mother and child. The child is becoming harder to manage. No longer is the child content to follow his/her mother's every wish. A separate will starts to emerge as the child begins separating from the psyche of the mother. The stiffening response is seen more often than the molding response, typical of the oneness that was prevalent only a month before. Some mothers thrive on the oneness stage and, for them, the stiffening response is threatening. Other mothers are relieved that the period of intense neediness and dependency may be soon ending. In either case, many mothers are confused and angry at times by these shifts in behavior from oneness to separateness.

The pressures on mothers during these early days are often increased by murky feelings and memories of their own infancy or childhood. She can feel like a failure as a mother of her baby and as the baby of her mother. Resentment at not getting her own needs met as an infant can make it difficult indeed to give freely to her own baby. Then she may feel guilty for not wanting to give freely, which in turn usually leads to more resentment. If the mother denies her feelings, they can easily build into bitterness and rage. Also, some mothers have too much pride to ask for help when they need it, making matters even worse.

Mothers who have the support of an understanding husband or partner usually can maneuver through these murky waters without damaging themselves or the child. Frequently, the husband is not all that supportive because he, too, may have unintegrated feelings and memories surfacing, perhaps feeling reduced in importance by this intruder or getting jealous of the special closeness and bonding of mother and child. This may trigger old sibling rivalry issues from his childhood where he felt reduced in importance by the arrival of a newborn brother or sister. (The father certainly isn't a central figure in the development of oneness, but his importance in the completion of the separateness phase will be discussed later.)

The five-month-old child has little time for anger or hatred. He/she is still lovingly focused on the experience of shared goodness. Children at this age see their mother as a saintly Madonna and see themselves as an angel. Soon the child will learn that there are limits to this perfect love, and he/she will begin to hate the mother when she isn't always there to make him/her feel wonderful and whole. If this illusion of perfection breaks down too quickly, the child may also believe that he/she did something wrong to cause the mother not to be there, and thus a devaluing of self can be the result rather than an understanding of the limitations of this primal trust relationship.

Babies know when to start separating, but several variables either speed up or slow down the process. When mothers are depressed, overtired or unavailable, their babies delay separating, somehow knowing that they must strengthen the sense of oneness before they can move toward separateness. In the case of clinging mothers, a baby will move toward separateness as quickly as possible. Such babies may even show a preference for strangers as early as three months and will stiffen against their mother's attempt to pick them up.

When babies begin this process of separation, they usually have two mothers for a while: a mother of oneness and a mother of separation. The mother of oneness waits, watches and stays in one place where her baby can easily find her. The mother of separation does not sit and wait, but goes about her business still making sure her baby knows where she is. She also helps arrange an environment for her baby that is safe but stimulating. She encourages her baby to reach out and allows the baby to play alone in her presence. Some mothers have trouble being mothers of separation, and they hover and intrude too often in these beginning stages.

Early Conquest

From about five months to eleven months, babies engage in a process of creeping away and then returning to their mother. It is a time of intense learning and growing. Never again will the child grow and learn so much in a short time span. As far as physical growth is concerned, from birth to ten months, the child will triple in weight and be eight to nine inches taller. The child will learn a million things about "what is me and what is not me." Some of the most important developmental learnings include:

1. creeping, crawling and standing
2. grabbing, pinching, tearing, pulling, scratching, biting, chewing and tasting everything that is "not me" in the environment
3. becoming an active participant in feeding and eating
4. becoming rageful, if necessary
5. holding an image of an object even when the object is not present
6. trusting other people in addition to mother

The Love Affair with the World

About the time they learn to stand and walk, usually about ten to twelve months, the toddler develops a "love affair with the world." The object of the toddler's wishes now shifts from mother to the world. At first there is so much to do out there that the toddler barely misses his or her mother, until something unexpected or frightening occurs, and then he/she will still want a mother or father there to comfort and soothe the hurt parts. However, there is a magical sense that mother is everywhere and will protect him/her. The toddler will spend the next several months perfecting movements and skills he or she had practiced earlier. The toddler wants nothing more than to get better at climbing, carrying, jumping, walking, turning in circles and naming things.

If mother is too uptight and intrudes too much or the opposite, if mother leaves the child alone too much, the toddler may not be able to experience this love affair fully and freely. Also there are different expectations for boys and girls. Mothers tend to encourage their sons to run about and be more physical in their exploration, while for girls it is a different story. Mothers worry more about the physical safety of their daughters, even though, developmentally, girls are physically stronger and more coordinated than boys at the same age. As a result, girls hold back and may not experience the full grandeur of their love affair with the world.

Low-Keyedness

At about fifteen months or so, a period of low-keyedness develops. During this time, the toddler turns inward once more, seemingly mourning the temporary loss of the oneness. There is some reality to this, for while the toddler is happily engaged in loving the world, mother is able to slip away more and more without notice. Mother goes out for an afternoon or an evening and returns to find her toddler leaping into her arms in tears or running toward her and then turning away. This period of low-keyedness is actually preparation for the real letdown that will occur when the love affair comes to an end. Toddlers begin to be aware of their limitations and aloneness in the world. They realize that they are not going to be able to conquer the world. They realize that, for all their efforts, they are still small, vulnerable, helpless and needy.

Frequently, at about eighteen months to two years, toddlers make another attempt to heal their wounded narcissism. The way they choose is to coerce mother back into a state of oneness and hope that this time they will get mirrored enough to go on with the separateness process. The toddler uses a number of ways to try to get mother's attention, including temper tantrums, whining, acting like mother in play and acting depressed.

Splitting

During this period, the "splitting" phenomenon occurs. When mother is available and meets all the child's needs she becomes a "good mother," and when she is busy or not available to meet the child's needs, she becomes "bad mother." It is difficult for a child of this age to hold on to the good part while experiencing the bad part. The role of the father is crucial in getting this conflict resolved. For boys, it is essential that they dis-identify with mother and have a father to whom they can attach. This actually starts at about one year of age. This provides them with enough emotional distance from their mother to begin to see her more objectively as having both good and bad qualities. Fathers have to support their sons during these times against the "bad mother" until this gets resolved. If fathers are absent or non-supportive, then the child cannot separate from mother and also cannot resolve the splitting problem. Boys who don't resolve the problem also have great difficulty identifying with men. They may do masculine things, but it is always to earn the love or approval of a mother figure.

Girls tend to remain tied to their mothers longer. Girls usually don't imitate the behavior of their fathers. Gradually during the separation phase of the second birth, girls turn toward their fathers for some of the nurturing and admiration they formerly sought exclusively from mother. If fathers respond lovingly, girl toddlers believe they don't have to be like mother to get validated as a person. If fathers ignore or turn away from their daughter's attempts to have their selfhood validated, then they fear they have to be more like mother in order to get more love from their father. The fear becomes "Can I be a girl without having to be like my mother?" or "Can I exist if I am not a mother?" Some adult women who got stuck in that stage are compulsively driven to become mothers so they can validate their selfhood.

Fathers must take an active role in resolving the separateness issue for both boys and girls. If the father withdraws or becomes hypercritical toward the mother, it impedes the process. In the latter situation, it serves notice to the child that mother is a dangerous creature and makes it even more difficult for the child to separate from her. Some never do separate. The father's role in this process is to be able to empathize with his wife's struggle, to see her occasional frantic and sometimes inconsistent behavior as a normal reaction to being a mother. He needs to offer support, not criticism. For the child, the father must also be able to freely offer masculine support and tenderness, sometimes protecting the child from a perceived "bad mother." Without a father's active involvement at this stage, the second birth cannot get completed, and many lifelong struggles are set in motion as people try to complete their psychological birth later, as adults.

Generally, people who haven't completed this process have low object constancy and are easily shattered by life's letdowns and disappointments. Frequently, these people are stuck in co-dependent patterns that lead them to idealize their relationship partners, hoping in this way to regain object constancy. This strategy always fails because their partners are just ordinary people who aren't able to perform superhuman feats and who do not wish to be controlled by the other. The overvaluing can then easily turn to undervaluing, and the once all-perfect partner can be disposed of as a worthless nothing. This also leads us to see ourselves as all bad, which requires us to search frantically for another perfect partner to help cover up these inner fears and vulnerabilities. This splitting of the world into all good and all bad is the basis for all comparative thinking. Some people can only measure their own worth by comparing themselves with someone else. These people have a difficult time experiencing genuine intimacy with another person, because intimacy requires a leveling or equal relationship.

As we look again at the completion of the oneness and separateness process, we find that very few people are able to complete their psychological birth on schedule. They get stuck somewhere in the process, perhaps due to a lack of mirroring early in the process, or due to the absence of a supportive father later in the process. One thing is for sure—the drive to complete this most important developmental task never ceases. It is the driving force behind all your attempts to work out your family patterns and why you continue to reexperience your unresolved issues over and over again in your adult relationships. Until we can help more parents to better understand and identify with the needs of their children, plus help parents learn to deal with their own narcissistic wounds in constructive ways, we will likely not advance the cause of humanity much further than it now is. Parents do not need extensive psychological training, however, only a few commonsense rules:

1. Remember the respect and tolerance you had for your own parents when you were a child and provide that same respect and tolerance for your children.

2. Refrain from using your children to satisfy your own needs.

3. Become aware of what in you got broken during childhood and then take the necessary steps to fix it.

4. Strive to learn as much as you can from your children about A) their world of childhood; B) the nature of the child within each of us and C) the nature of feelings, which can be observed more easily in children.

5. Allow your children to express the full range of their feelings without threats of loss of love or physical harm.

Awareness Activity

One way to personalize the information about human development is to go back and try to recall your earliest memory. Describe it as completely as you can, including what you saw, heard, felt, smelled, tasted, intuited, and what you think you might have concluded about yourself, other people and the world as a result of the experience.

Also describe all the actions you can remember, who else was there, what everyone said and did, etc. After writing out as complete a description as possible, read the description to a friend and ask them to give you feedback on what they think a person with that memory might have concluded about him/herself, other people and/or the world around them. Check out what your friend tells you to see if there was a decision that you may have made at that time that may have set a pattern for your life.

I remember doing this activity with a client who told me that her earliest memory was seeing herself sitting by herself on the grass when she was about two years old. She remembered looking around, but no one was there. She said she felt lonely and confused but she wasn't crying. As she finished telling me that part, she burst into tears with deep sobs. I comforted her and, when she could talk again, she said she realized that she had already decided not to cry so she wouldn't upset her parents, no matter how lonely and confused she got. This, she realized, was the beginning of a life pattern of taking care of others and denying her own needs (a parentized child). By knowing the source of her brokenness, she gradually began to change her co-dependent pattern by learning to identify and actively get her own needs met.

Betrayal and the Path of the Heart

precious mom (handwritten)

James Hillman (1975) presents a penetrating analysis of the concept of betrayal. Betrayal, according to Hillman, enables you to grow out of your total dependence on the concept of primal trust as the basis for your adult relationships, which for all its merits, still can keep you trapped in infancy. Under the spell of primal trust, first experienced as part of the bonding process with your mother, you tend to maintain a fairly ego-centered, limited view of your relationships. In this view, everyone behaves according to the way you would like them to behave. As a young child, you believed in this make–believe condition where you saw the world and other significant people in your life as always fair and just and existing to serve all your needs. As unreal as this premise is, most people grow up still trying to make a primal trust work for them in their adult relationships.

Even during childhood, this premise probably broke down and your primal trust in your parents was shattered. They turned out not to be superhuman deities, but ordinary fallible creatures who could not be trusted to do what you wanted them to do most of the time. As a result, you survived childhood with a multitude of battle scars and wounds, all received in the name of primal trust.

As an adult, you certainly should understand the limits of primal trust as a basis for relationship, but you don't seem to. Instead, what you are most likely to do is to try to create an adult relationship based on primal trust. You are still trying to return to the state of oneness and perfection you experienced ever so briefly during early childhood, which is much more transcendent and God-like than human. The illusion of primal trust allows you to believe that you can become like God and can control your relationship, rising above or transcending the limitations unfairly imposed on you by your humanness. When this primal trust begins to break down in your adult relationships, you experience it as a betrayal by someone you trusted. Despite the problems and pain it causes, betrayal provides you with the opportunity or challenge to become fully human and to understand how to operate in the world as a complete human being.

In those moments when you experience your greatest letdowns, you are given an opportunity to grow from your experience, to expand your limited view of the world or to fall back, as it were, into what Hillman calls the "sterile choices." The sterile choices are revenge, denial, cynicism, paranoia and self-betrayal. Each one of these choices is described briefly below. Please note that none of these choices leads to growth or new awareness.

Revenge is reflected in the old Biblical adage "an eye for an eye and a tooth for a tooth." It is a natural response to being hurt by hurting back. Temporarily you may feel good, if you can even the score. However, the long-term effects are usually counter-revenge and more feuding. It merely breeds more of the same and consequently becomes all-consuming. If you delay your revenge, as you often do, you start plotting, sneaking around, lying low and sinking further into self-defeating cruelty and vindictiveness where you start "cutting off your nose to spite your face." This is the basis for the vicious cycle of cruelty.

The next limiting response to betrayal is *denial*. If you are betrayed by a loved one, you are tempted to deny the value of the other person and see only their evil ways. You somehow cast a shadow over everything this person stands for. Because you failed again in your efforts to realize your great hope for a relationship, which is growing together in mutual ways with duration, you turn away from a relationship and deny your hopes and expectations. You may say, "Never again will I be so stupid as to get into a relationship," or "All men are _____" or, "All women are _____."

An even more damaging response to betrayal is cynicism. Your

89

disappointments in love, with an organization, a cause, a friend, a boss or a therapist can lead you to deny the value of the other and this leads you to coldness and hardness. "All love is worthless, causes are for dreamers, organizations for conformists and therapists for weaklings." You decide you won't trust anyone again and you will just play it cool. From this position you again feel safe, but it becomes a betrayal to your self and your ideals, dreams and ambitions. It is a stuck place where we cannot see any of the positive elements of life.

Cynicism always seems to lead you to *self-betrayal* if it is not processed. In a trust relationship, you allowed yourself to be vulnerable and open. In this position you often utter a confession, write a love letter or a poem or reveal a secret, a childhood dream or a fear. As a result of some betrayal of that trust, you start to devalue yourself. The love letter becomes sentimental rubbish and the other things you shared are boring, ridiculous crap. When you are betrayed, you are handed over to the enemy within, who has a field day with your hurts. You do not want to hurt that way again, and since your hurt came as a result of revealing yourself, you decide to withdraw yourself from life. You refuse to be who you are, and you may fall into what Jung called "uneigentlich leiden," the inauthentic life. In this condition, you likely will deliver low-level "schlock" kicks to yourself and fall further away from purposeful living.

There is one other sterile choice, which Hillman calls the *paranoid* choice. When you make this choice, you may attempt to protect yourself by creating a fail-safe relationship. You may agree to enter another relationship *only* if the other agrees to take an oath never to betray. You may require proof of complete devotion, declarations of everlasting fidelity and built-in checks and periodic tests for no possibility of a slip. This kind of relationship has limited growth potential, and love usually withers under the intense scrutiny of the fearful one.

Let us look now at the possibility of making a choice other than the ones presented. At the most basic level, you can look at betrayal as an opportunity to expand your concept of reality. Before you were betrayed, you lived under an illusion of the way you thought things were, and as a result of your betrayal, you discovered that things were not the way you thought they were. Everybody has dreams of the way we would like our life, relationships, parents and job to be. We block out those parts of our reality that don't fit with our dreams.

For example, the wife with an alcoholic husband dreams that someday he will reform and stop drinking if she only can love him enough and make him feel worthwhile enough. This woman will likely endure tremendous pain and abuse before she gives up her dream. Often some betrayal occurs that shocks her into a new awareness, and she finally lets go of her dream. She now has an opportunity to expand her reality. If she does just that, she guarantees that she most likely will not have to be betrayed in the same way again. She will have learned a valuable, although costly, lesson. However, the cost increases even more when you fail to learn these lessons and you have to go through a similar, costly betrayal again. Betrayals provide you with an opportunity to advance your consciousness.

At a higher level, you have an opportunity to become conscious of and to integrate your own unintegrated parts that led you into a betrayal. Frequently we deny our own jealousy or anger or sadness and 'try' to be nice. Only by accepting your situations and feelings will you be able to grow psychologically through the process of betrayal. Betrayal gives you the opportunity to see yourself more fully, particularly those parts of your behavior that are outside of your awareness.

If you go one step further, you may reach one of the highest religious/spiritual feelings: forgiveness. Forgiveness only becomes a real possibility if you have truly experienced betrayal. At times you can forgive a petty insult or personal affront, but when you have bared your soul in a trust relationship and then been deeply betrayed, you can begin to understand the difficulty of choosing forgiveness as an option. Forgiveness in this context involves a process of fully seeing yourself and the other, not as you would like to see or be seen but exactly as you are. True forgiveness does not deny anger, it faces it head on. If you can feel the outrage of betrayal and recognize what was done to you and actually feel hatred toward your betrayer for what he or she did to you, then the path to forgiveness is more open to you. It involves no denial, no wishing it away, no magical incantations, only *an honest accounting of who you are and who that other person really is, including the limitations and failings of yourself and the betrayer.* It also includes an empathy for the other because of the recognition of your own limitations and failings. This full recognition of self and other is probably as close as you can come to agape or brotherly/sisterly love. Frequently, you can deepen your love and understanding for others only after betrayal becomes a part of your relationship.

Although trust certainly has held a revered place in your life, in order to grow up you must also make a place in your life for betrayal. You were conceived through a wounding of the egg by the sperm, and so your consciousness is conceived and grows through a wounding of your primal trust by the betrayer. You were wounded, first by your parents and later by others with whom you formed close relationships.

This leaves you with one unanswered question: Who is the betrayer? And what is the lesson for the betrayer? Actually, your betrayer is inside of you and is the unintegrated part of you that fails to see certain elements of reality and that helps draw the actual betrayer to you and contributes to setting up the betrayal situation. For men, their unintegrated part is usually their unintegrated feminine side projected outward onto a woman who eventually betrays them. For women, their unintegrated part is often their masculine side and usually gets projected onto a man who eventually betrays them. Because of this, two people in a relationship can both experience betrayal at the same time.

For example, a woman who has not integrated her own power may draw a man into her life who she dreams is someone who uses his masculine power to get what he wants. She may dream that by being with him she will learn how to become more powerful, only to find that he becomes a betrayer as well and uses his power to put her down. At the same time, the betrayer may not want to use his power the way he does and is dreaming that this woman, who he sees as more loving, will show him how to become more loving. His dream also is threatened when he finds out that she often acts more like a helpless victim than a loving companion, until he finally feels frustrated enough to pull a power-play and feels betrayed again by a woman.

The lesson for the betrayer, therefore, is the same as that of the betrayed. As a betrayer, you can also utilize the sterile choices to avoid your lessons, or you can use the betrayal situation to take back and begin to integrate your previously unintegrated parts. In the role of the betrayer, you first have to wake up from the dream and look at your reality in a new way. Only then can you forgive yourself completely enough to approach the betrayed person with the necessary openness to bring about a resolution. If you have forgiven yourself, then you can admit your mistake and ask for forgiveness from the betrayed and even allow the betrayed person to have his or her feelings of anger, sadness or fear.

A resolution cannot be reached by avoiding the issue, the betrayed person involved or the feelings involved. The word *forgiveness* means to *give back* or *take back*. In the case of self-forgiveness, it refers to taking back that which belongs to you and taking ownership or responsibility for your part in the betrayal. This includes giving back the projections you have of the other and taking back your own projections. In this way, betrayal assists both the betrayer and the betrayed to grow in individual consciousness and in relationship.

Awareness Activity

Begin this activity by making a list of the significant betrayals you have experienced in your life. You can make the list chronological, starting with the earliest one you can remember, or you can arrange your list from the most significant down to the least significant. After you have listed all these events (you only need a few words like "the time that . . ." happened), go back over them and examine: 1) the feelings you had at the time and the feelings you have now, 2) which choice you made and 3) what the lesson was to be learned in betrayal. Also ask yourself what other important benefits came out of the betrayal for you and the others involved. Finally, what are the patterns of betrayal that are woven through the various betrayal events? Are your betrayers mostly men or women? Were they older or younger than you? Have certain kinds of betrayal occurred more than once? Which betrayals have you successfully healed? Which have you not healed? What do you plan to do with those that are not healed?

After you have completed the above parts of the activity, go back and do it again, this time from the standpoint of the betrayer. Make a list of the times where you were the betrayer and betrayed someone else. Be honest with yourself. Most people can more easily remember the times when they were betrayed rather than the times when they betrayed others.

An Example of a Betrayal

John and Nancy are a very loving couple who have been married for almost ten years. When they came to therapy, they were experiencing

93

a real crisis in their marriage. John had just admitted to Nancy that he was having a sexual relationship with another woman he had met at work. Nancy had sensed that something was wrong because he was spending more time at work in the evenings. Their sexual relationship had tapered off, but she never allowed herself to dream that John would betray her in this way. She imagined that John would always be faithful to her and that his moodiness was just due to pressure at work. John said he had become dissatisfied with his sexual relationship with Nancy because they were always doing things the same way. He found it hard to talk to Nancy about his dissatisfaction because he thought she would be too embarrassed. Also he began to doubt his own sexuality since he sometimes had trouble holding his erection.

Gradually he withdrew from Nancy and began to look for reassurance from a female co-worker who he often met for lunch. Eventually, John began to take a romantic interest in his friend and they started a sexual relationship. Then he began to experience guilt and remorse but felt trapped. He had to lie to Nancy now to deal with his affair, and this increased his guilt and his need to withdraw from Nancy. Finally this became unbearable for John and he confessed to Nancy what had been happening. Nancy was hurt deeply by this betrayal and at first wanted to get revenge for what John did to her. She moved out for a week, staying with a girl friend, but she then decided to ask John to go for counseling with her to sort out the problems. In the course of therapy, John was able to express his sexual needs directly to Nancy, and Nancy was able to ask John to spend more time with her instead of at work. The openness with which they were able to express and listen to each other's feelings had increased greatly during their time in therapy, and they were able to deepen their relationship with each other. They came to see how this crisis had happened and began to take steps to make it less likely that they would have to repeat that betrayal again.

In this case, the betrayal brought many unresolved issues to the surface and allowed them to be resolved. When one or both people in a relationship are holding on to a dream about the other person or the relationship, usually some betrayal is necessary to shatter the dream and help them expand their reality.

CHAPTER TEN

Life Before Birth

> *We now know that the unborn child
> is an aware, reacting human
> being....*
> —THOMAS VERNY

Only in the past twenty years have we developed the necessary technology to study the life of the unborn child. We have always been fascinated by stories about how we can influence later development of the child by the books the mother reads or the music she listens to or her messages to her unborn child, but any reported effects have usually been dismissed by medical science as old wives' tales or crazy projections. Now with the development of tiny ultra-sensitive sensors and sound equipment, medical science can better study the world of the unborn child. Specific research has now confirmed many of the old wives' tales and discovered that the unborn child is far more developed than we ever imagined. For example, studies have shown that by the fifth week of fetal development, the child has already acquired a complex set of reflex actions. By the eighth week, the child is moving its head, arms and trunk with ease and has already developed a primitive body language usually expressed in deliberate jerks or kicks. (Verny 1981)

Boys Will Be Boys

We have known for some time that from conception until the twelfth week, the sex of the fetus is female. If a male child is going to develop, drastic changes start about the twelfth week and continue until the time of birth. These changes disrupt the flow of development of the male fetus, while disruptions are not experienced by the female fetus. Because of this developmental disruption, girl babies are developmentally advanced over boy babies at birth, and this developmental gap increases and continues until about age sixteen. This gap between boys and girls can be as much as one year or two years during this time. This may account for the fact that almost ninety percent of all birth defects and genetic abnormalities occur in males, and eighty percent of all infant crib deaths are male children. Young male children often suffer untold damages to their self-esteem because of their inability to match the performance levels of female babies, who usually crawl, walk, talk and respond earlier than male babies.

Male children learn that they cannot get the rewards that come from being able to please parents by their performance, so they often settle for another kind of reward from the negative attention they get when they displease parents by their performance. There is actually a positive side to this dilemma, because in order to displease parents, male children have to think of ways to get their parents' attention. Female children, because they so easily meet parental expectations and easily get external rewards such as praise, smiles, being picked up and getting hugged, *do not have to think* about how to do it and therefore become classically conditioned to external rewards. Later this can cause problems for girls and women because they have trouble thinking about their wants and needs and ways they can actively meet them. Boys and men may also get conditioned to negative rewards from parental attention and contact, but because they engaged in more thinking in order to get these rewards, later they are better able to think of their needs and ways to get them met.

In addition, our public school system makes no provision for these developmental differences, requiring boys and girls of the same age to be in the same grades and learn at the same rate. As a result, over eighty percent of the children labeled as having learning disabilities in school who are often placed in special education classes are males. Even higher percentages of males show up in special Emotional-Behavioral Disturbance classes. We have not even begun to fully comprehend the long-term effects of placing male children in a one-down position, in comparison to females, for their first sixteen years of life. Perhaps this is the time bomb that explodes later in crimes of violence against women, children and society. Perhaps it is also behind male alcoholism and drug abuse patterns where the anger is turned inward. We need to do much more research on this topic, since it also applies to the narcissistic wounding and the vicious cycle of cruelty.

Early Signs of Development

By the fourth month, the unborn child can frown, squint and grimace. If the child's eyelids are touched, it will squint and if the child's lips are touched, it will start sucking. By the sixth month, the child is as sensitive to touch as a one-year-old. The child will kick violently if cold water is injected into the amniotic fluid. Also, by this time the child has developed a good sense of taste. If saccharin is added to the amniotic fluid, the child's rate of swallowing responses doubles, while the addition of a foul-tasting, iodine-like substance will cause the rate to drop, and the child develops facial grimaces as well.

From the sixth month on, the child listens all the time and a pregnant woman's abdomen and uterus are indeed noisy places. The loudest sounds that the unborn child hears are its mother's stomach rumblings. Voices of the mother, father and others are also audible to the unborn. The mother's regular heartbeat is the constant sound that lets the unborn child know that all is well. Perhaps this is why later a small child can be lulled to sleep by the ticking of a clock. Some researchers found that when adults were asked to set a metronome at the rate that pleased them most, they chose fifty to ninety beats per minute—the range of the human heartbeat. Some people believe that our musical talents are awakened in the womb by the rhythms of our mother's heartbeat. Studies have shown that unborn children prefer the largo beat (sixty beats per minute) to rock music, which causes them to kick violently. (Verny 1984)

Vision develops more slowly in the darkness of the womb. However, from the sixteenth week on, the unborn child can be easily startled by shining a light directly on the mother's stomach. At birth the child is dreadfully myopic but has excellent vision at six to twelve inches, which is the distance from the mother's breast to the mother's face.

Early Signs of Consciousness and Memory

The early sensory development is necessary for learning to occur. Recent research (Verny 1981) has confirmed that consciousness exists

97

from the twenty-eighth week on. By that time, the cerebral cortex is as advanced as that of a newborn, so thinking, feeling and remembering are possible from then on. Brain waves become distinct from the thirty-second week on and even REM (Rapid Eye Movement) sleep patterns can be detected, which suggests that dreaming may be occurring.

Subjects in LSD research by Stan Grof (1976) reported clear memories from the womb that were verified as accurate. Other researchers have looked at the emotional life of the unborn child through follow-up studies of children who, while in an unborn state, were exposed to marital strife between their mother and father.

In a study of over thirteen hundred children and their families, one researcher (Scott 1973) showed that ". . . a woman locked in a stormy marriage runs a 237 percent greater risk of bearing a psychologically or physically damaged child than a woman in a secure, nurturing relationship." This risk actually rated higher than other recognized risks, such as physical illness, smoking or the performance of back-breaking labor during pregnancy. The research showed that unhappy marriages produced babies who were five times more fearful and jumpy than children from happy marriages. At the age of four or five, these children are undersized, timid and highly dependent on their mothers.

Another long-term, follow-up study showed similar results. This group of researchers at the Fels Research Institute tested unborn babies for changes in heart rate when an external stimuli was introduced (a loud noise made near the mother). They hoped to see those identified as having few changes in heart rate (low reactors) would maintain this personality trait long after birth. They found that when these children were tested in the same way fifteen years later, they still exhibited few changes in heart rate when a loud noise was made. The group of high reactors showed equally persistent patterns of over reaction to a loud noise. Another interesting finding of this study (Sontag 1963) was that the high reactors were more creative and better able to identify feelings in themselves and others than were those in the low reactor group who tended to be much more concrete.

Several other recent studies have confirmed that mothers who consciously and subconsciously wanted to be pregnant produced much healthier babies, emotionally and physically, at birth and afterward than those mothers who did not want to be pregnant. One of these studies produced another interesting result. One group of mothers consciously said they wanted to be pregnant but through psychological tests were shown to not really want to be pregnant. The offspring of these mothers seemed to know this subconscious reality and, as a result, had an unusually large number of behavioral and gastrointestinal problems.

In the same study, another group of mothers was identified as having many doubts and fears about being pregnant, but the psychological tests showed that despite the conscious doubts and fears, they really wanted to be pregnant. Children from these mothers seemed to pick up both messages and were confused. At birth, an unusually large number of these children were apathetic and lethargic. (Verny 1981)

These studies are just the beginning, for there is so much still to know about prenatal development and its effects on later development. Each of these studies answers some limited questions but leaves many more questions to answer.

During Grof's LSD research, hypnotherapy and breath-work clients could describe events from their unborn state in great detail. Some even reported a memory trace of their own conception. We do know that much of what we had previously labeled as old wives' tales turned out to be accurate statements about the ability of mothers to influence the subsequent development of their children while still in the womb. If I were pregnant (which I never can be), I think I would do everything I could to provide positive emotional, physical and intellectual experiences for my unborn child. I would read to it, talk to it, sing to it, eat good food for it, play music to it and anything else I could think of to provide a positive climate for the development of my unborn infant.

CHAPTER ELEVEN

The Impact of the Birth Trauma And the Bonding Process

You can't pay anyone to do what a mother will do for free.
—RUSSIAN PROVERB

Until recently, most obstetrical practices were designed to get the birth process over as quickly as possible. It was thought that the longer the process took, the more likely that something might go wrong. To support this expedient approach was the belief that the newborn infant had a very underdeveloped sensory system, and therefore the delivery room should be set up for the comfort of everyone but the newborn, who had very little awareness of the environment anyway. Based on this belief, male children were usually circumcised soon after birth without the use of anesthetics. Then new research evidence on the consciousness and sensory development of newborns began to totally refute this belief. Newborns were found to be very alert (particularly when the mother did not receive drugs during the delivery) and were found to have highly developed sensory awareness. In fact, what they found was that the newborn infant's senses were acutely sensitive at birth to such things as bright lights, loud noises and cold temperatures.

Even with this overwhelming evidence, obstetrical practices were very slow to change. Pioneers such as the French obstetrician, Frederick LeBoyer, began to develop new, more humane birthing practices, allowing the child to be born in dimmed lights, with soft music and whispering attendants. LeBoyer also believed in allowing the child to breathe on its own before cutting the umbilical cord. In addition, he bathed and massaged the child right after birth in warm water the same temperature as the womb, as well as allowing much skin-to-skin contact between mother and child and even father and child. The medical profession ridiculed his practices and held fast to the old ways. Despite all the research evidence and the development of new humane birthing practices that are supported by the research, many children in civilized countries are still being birthed in the traditional way.

These practices are gradually being forced to change because many parents are taking birthing matters into their own hands and refusing to go to hospitals for delivery. Home births, sometimes assisted by a physician or a midwife, are becoming increasingly popular, even though some states have laws prohibiting the use of midwives in the birthing process. Some states have passed licensing laws for midwives to regulate their practice by undergoing special training. This has become an economic issue and hospitals have had to develop birthing centers that are warm and home-like and allow the mother, child and father to stay together following the birth process. Also, more hospitals are developing LeBoyer's birthing procedures to meet the demand.

There is a sense among those who work extensively with birthing that we have only begun to come out of the dark ages in relation to birth practices.

The author is personally aware of one such experiment under-way by a group of people who do not wish to be identified at this time. They are attempting to work with couples at least a year prior to the couple's desired conception date. The couple is led through a physical, emotional and spiritual purification program designed to prepare them to consciously conceive a child. They then work with the couple during the pregnancy to provide the most stress-free, enriched environment possible to influence the prenatal and the later perinatal development of the child. They provide mother and child with meditation, massage, yoga and swimming exercises. They have mother and unborn child listen to beautiful music and provide them with artistic media to stimulate thoughts and attitudes of peace and tranquility. They also encourage couples to utilize floatation tanks for stress reduction and increased communication between parents and the unborn child.

At the time of birth, the couple is allowed to choose the environment and style of birth they prefer. Some children in this program

101

have actually been born underwater. Following the birth, they encourage the mothers and newborns to play for hours in a water environment. This almost gravity-free environment allows newborns to move and develop their otherwise immobile bodies. This phase of their program is based on the work of Dr. Igor Charkovsky, a Russian obstetrician, who has discovered innovative developmental techniques using water environments that help babies grow and develop much faster and more completely than with ordinary methods. Dr. Charkovsky's work, which spans over twenty-five years, is still virtually unknown outside of Russia, but films showing his techniques are being used to help mothers and newborns during the first three months after birth.

This project is still in its infancy (pardon the pun), but it is the kind of project that could show us how to recognize and deal with the enormous privilege and responsibility we have in the positive evolution of our species.

Understanding Your Own Birth Trauma

Do you know under what conditions you were born? More than likely, you were born in a hospital under the following conditions. Pay close attention to your reactions as you read these words describing the standard obstetrical practices used in most hospitals: You have been floating blissfully in a pool of warm amniotic fluid when suddenly you are thrust into the birth canal and begin a traumatic experience that can last for hours. You feel pushed and pinched by your mother's contractions as you are being moved down the birth canal. When your head nears the vaginal opening, your fragile skull may be seized on each side of the head by two steel forceps, still used in over thirty percent of births, and pulled forward at a force equal to forty pounds of tension on your neck. You may also have a metal electrode lead from a fetal heart monitor inserted under your scalp (now used routinely by some obstetricians). Your birth process is also made more difficult for both you and your mother by having her lie flat on her back with her feet in stirrups, going against the natural forces of gravity.

Finally, you emerge from the birth canal into a cold, noisy world of bright lights and tense people in masks. You likely have been drugged, over-stressed and are exhausted. Before you have an opportunity to rest and begin breathing on your own, the umbilical cord is cut, you are hooked up to a respirator or held up by your heels and slapped on the back. Already exhausted from your ordeal, you now have suction devices stuck in your mouth, nose and ears, your eyelids are peeled back, letting in painful light, and even more painful chemicals are put in your tender eyes.

Then you are rubbed clean to remove the blood from your mother's episiotomy and you are laid on cold, hard scales to be weighed like a choice roast of beef. To make matters even worse, you are then wrapped tightly in a blanket and whisked away from your mother, who may not have even had a chance to see you. You may be placed in a nursery or incubator, either screaming in pain and terror or semiconscious from the anesthesia administered to your mother during the birth process.

It might be possible to overcome some of this trauma if it weren't for one more barbaric act that is almost impossible to overstate. You were totally isolated from your mother. No court of justice could hand out a punishment severe enough to balance this crime against a helpless child. This isolation cancels every possible chance for bonding, for relaxation of the birth stress ". . . and for the completion of the reticular formation for full mental, physical coordinates and learning." (Pearce 1977:58) These very specific processes connected to birth are missed and somehow must be laboriously rebuilt later. As a result of this trauma, there is virtually no development possible until the effects of the birth trauma are reduced by the development of the warm, nurturing bond between mother and child, which may already have been damaged severely.

Even though you may not have felt any connections with the birth process described above, it is important to get as much information about your birth as possible. If your mother is still alive you can ask her, but she may have been drugged and will have to find out from others who were present. Having this information may help you trace any unexplained behavior patterns back to something connected to your birth.

The following questions are important to ask:

1. What were the conditions of the delivery table? Were there any complications? Was it air-conditioned? Noisy? Were bright lights used? How many people were present? Was my father there?

2. How long did the delivery take? Were there any complica-

tions? If so, how were these handled? Were forceps used? What kind of anesthetic was used? Was the umbilical cord cut immediately? Was I held up by the heels and smacked on the back to induce breathing?

3. How much contact did I have with my mother and father immediately after birth? Did my mother nurse me? For how long?

4. If you are a circumcised male, ask: When was it done? Was an anesthetic used?

5. What other stories or incidental information can people tell me about my birth?

Sometimes by getting more complete information about your birth, you can begin to see relationships and connections not immediately apparent before.

We don't actually know what the long-term effects of this kind of birth experience are. We can only speculate. When Frederick Le-Boyer was asked on a television interview what other life events are as important as birth, he replied that there are no other important events—only the repeated experience of one's birth trauma until it is released. One seemingly long-term effect is what I call the "watch out" effect. This occurs when we are feeling very good and we get a thought that tells us to "watch out" for bad things to follow. We actually develop a personal quota of how long we can sustain our good feelings before our anxiety forces the good feelings away.

People who had a caesarean birth often have this "watch out" problem. Over fifteen percent of all births are done by caesarean section, and the figure has increased by some two hundred percent in the last two decades. (Kelly 1979) A long-term effect of caesarean delivery is an intense craving for all kinds of physical contact. The birth trauma may be more severe for a caesarean section baby because there is such an abrupt and rapid change from the womb to the external environment.

Other speculation involves the connections between back problems in adulthood and being slapped on the back to induce breathing. Chiropractors who pay attention to the possible causes of back problems report that this connection seems to be present in many of their patients. Whiplash injuries from being rear-ended while driving is another possible outcome from the birth trauma.

At a deeper level, we have evidence that the trauma of birth does seem to have deep psychological effects. Stanislav Grof (1976), in his research on the therapeutic use of LSD, found that many of his subjects were able to relive their birth experience and thus release the traumatic effects of their birth. He wrote that those subjects who were able to relive their birth experience and feel a release from the trauma stored in their body memory system also experienced the ". . . dramatic alleviation or disappearance of previous, psychopathological symptoms and a decrease of emotional problems of all kinds." He also noted that during the reliving of their birth experience they reported having ". . . feelings of enormous decompression and expansion of space." Finally, upon completion of the process, they reported feeling ". . . liberation, redemption, salvation, love and forgiveness."

Similar results have occurred in breath work with clients in my own practice. I do not use psychedelic drugs in my practice, but in teaching people to release stored psychological material from their bodies using the breath, many report a full recall of their birth experience, including the ability to know the thoughts and feelings of those present at their birth. The word psychotherapy, before it took on a medical meaning, meant *the process of working with breathing*.

One psychotherapy client, a woman in her mid-thirties, had been working on her conflicts with her father and her inability to have satisfactory relationships with men. I suggested that we might approach the problem through breath work. She rather reluctantly agreed, and I instructed her in the same breathing process I use to help release old patterns (see Chapter 15 for a complete description of this process). Following the session, she reported having complete recall of her birth, which was filled with complications endangering both mother and child. She was also able to recall what everybody present was thinking and feeling. She saw her father there, even though she didn't know he had been present, and then intuitively read his thoughts. "If someone has to die, let it be my child and not my wife." After sharing this with me she said, "That is why he has acted so guilty around me all these years; I never knew why."

The following day she called her father and told him what she had found out. He had actually forgotten the source of his guilt and resentment toward her, but when she told him the thoughts she had picked up, he was astonished because he then remembered having those exact thoughts at her birth. As a result of this insight, my client and her father were able to resolve their long-standing conflicts. She was able to forgive him for his thoughts and he forgave himself for having those thoughts.

In other breath–work sessions, clients have reported seeing a videotape with sound of their entire birth process. Other breath–work clients never have any recall of their birth, so it is hard to explain why it happens with some people and not others. Those who are successful with this technique seem to focus on a recall of childhood events or just experience a release in their body without knowledge of what they released. To those people who need to know what they've let go of, I often remind them that they don't have to examine each piece of garbage before taking it to the dump.

The Bonding Process

Despite study after study showing the importance of immediate bonding for mother and child, the still prevalent practice is to separate them immediately after the baby is born. Mothers and babies should have as much time together immediately after delivery as possible to allow for the vital bonding process to occur. This is necessary to 1) help release the tension in the child's muscles created during the birth process, 2) to fully activate the central nervous system and 3) to complete the reticular formations necessary for full mental and physical coordination. (Klaus & Kennell 1976)

A newborn baby, if allowed to, bonds or attaches almost immediately to his or her mother. The sound of her voice, the sight of her face during holding and feeding, the feel of her skin, the smell of her body, are all clear signals of safety and security for the newborn in this foreign and confusing world. To build this attachment, mother, father and child have to spend a significant amount of time together during the first twelve to twenty-four hours after birth, including skin-to-skin contact during the first hour or so after birth. The quality of this first attachment influences the quality of all other bonds and attachments we make during our lifetime.

Two researchers, Klaus and Kennell cited above (1976), have contributed much to our understanding of the bonding process. Their research findings are summarized in the following list of seven crucial components for the bonding process.

106

1. The optimal period for bonding is the first few minutes after birth through the first twelve hours. During this time, they suggest that both parents have maximum physical and sensory contact with the newborn.

2. The responses made by the mother or father immediately after the birth are necessary for the infant to activate its sensory attachments. They will remember their mother's voice later when asked to respond to other voices.

3. In multiple births, it was found that mother and father become attached to one child at a time. Each child needs time alone with its parents to maximize bonding.

4. The parents have to get some signal back from the infant to let them know the infant is responding to their attempts to bond. Otherwise, parents can get discouraged and withdraw from their infant, making the bonding more difficult.

5. Everyone present during the birth process will likely become attached to the infant. This would suggest that fathers and other immediate or extended family members should be allowed to be present at the birth, to make possible more attachments.

6. A newborn who has a life-threatening illness is difficult to bond with for most parents. They hold back and fear the feelings of loss should the child die. Also, fathers have trouble bonding with their children if their wife has life-threatening complications during the birth process.

7. The emotional condition of the parents (tense, relaxed, etc.) during the first few hours after the birth can have long-term effects on the child's development. For example, a mother who is overly anxious about the well-being of her child in the first day following the birth often maintains this over-anxious attitude and causes lasting effects to the mother-child relationship.

Long-Term Effects of Poor Bonding

Most of us who were probably deprived of the opportunities for full bonding might ask: "What are the long-term effects of poor bonding?" Again, we only have partial answers. We do know that neglect and physical as well as psychological abuse of infants are twice as high in parents who had their baby separated from them at birth during the optimal bonding period.

Safety is usually an issue for partially bonded children. Situations in which more fully bonded people might ask, "What is happening here?" the poorly bonded person might ask, "Am I safe here?" The concern for personal safety and survival often is so strong that partially bonded people evaluate an experience before they can incorporate that experience. They might say, for example, "I won't try to do that because it looks too hard." These people often restrict their lives so much to insure safety that they may become unhappy or jealous of others who seem to be able to do more things and have more fun.

Another problem for poorly bonded people is their inability to express anger. Their fear is that the expression of anger will destroy or weaken any bonding they have left. They often fear abandonment, and so they will do almost anything to avoid a problem that might cause someone close to leave them. Frequently, this anger is turned inward and forms a depression of energy and the development of degenerative disease.

One such person, Diane, came to me complaining of a rather bizarre set of physical symptoms including an intense burning in her chest, partial loss of hearing, dizziness, constipation and skin rashes. She also tended to maintain an overt attitude of superiority in her relationships. She had a recent physical exam that showed no apparent physical cause for these symptoms. They had to be psychosomatic in nature. In taking her history, I found out that she had been physically and sexually abused as a child. Her mother beat her and her father raped her when she was age six and then left the family. She truly believed that she was a bad person and that was why she was treated so poorly by her parents. She believed that somehow she caused her father to leave and was feeling very guilty.

Finally, I asked her about her birth. From what she had been told, her mother suffered complications during delivery and had almost died. She believed that it was several weeks before her mother actually saw her for the first time. She was told that her father came only to see her mother during those two weeks, and he was unable to face the possibility of his wife dying and having to raise a child alone. So during Diane's first two weeks of life, she experienced little or no bonding with either her mother or father. She said later that she felt closer to her father than she did to her mother. However, she identified so closely with her mother that she said when she looked in the mirror, she saw her mother's face and not her own.

I decided to work with her on building an identity separate from that of her mother. I asked her to make a list of the positive and negative ways she was the same as her mother and the ways she was not the same as her mother. The first list contained no traits that were different from her mother. Gradually she began to build a self-image that was somewhat different from that of her mother. I noticed that the more she was able to see herself that way, the more her physical symptoms would clear up. She also began to have more effective relationships in which she reported that she could be herself more. Occasionally her symptoms reappear, but they don't last as long anymore since she is better able to take care of herself. She will always have trouble with self-image and identity, particularly in close, intimate relationships. Now, rather than blame it on her partner, she may be able to understand it as the recurring bonding issue and therefore deal with it in more creative ways.

CHAPTER TWELVE

Unraveling Your Family Death Patterns

The only way out is through.
—Anonymous

Charles Dickens died at the age of fifty-eight; his son, Charles Culliford Dickens, died at the age of fifty-nine and his grandson, Charles Walter Dickens, died at the age of fifty-eight. Just a coincidence? I don't think so. I know of families, for example, where all males for the past four generations have died at age fifty-five of a heart attack; other families in which everyone dies of cancer at a certain age; and other families in which everyone is killed in an accident of one sort or another. Try a quick experiment. Ask yourself now: "At what age and how am I going to die?" Some number and a cause of death probably came into your mind, if you didn't quickly try to forget them. Where did you get those thoughts? Were you born with them? Probably not. You learned them from your family while you were growing up. Your bottom-line family pattern teaches you how to get sick, what illnesses to get and not get, and finally how and when to die. You might quickly check out these patterns in your family. It is helpful to include at least three and perhaps four generations. Find out:

1. What are the illnesses common to the members of your family?
2. What thoughts or family messages do you think might con-

tribute to people getting these illnesses? (Example: "We Devonshires are prone to sinus problems.")

3. At what ages do members of your family die? What patterns show up across three and four generations?

4. What are the common causes of death to members of your family? Again check across three to four generations.

Death is not controlled by our physical body; it is controlled by our unconscious thoughts, perceptions and beliefs, which tell our body how to do it. If you remember in Chapter 1, we talked about how people act on their perception of reality rather than reality itself. All of our family patterns belong to the category of perceptions of reality that are passed on from generation to generation without awareness. Only when you become consciously aware of these perceptions and patterns can you then change them. If you don't become conscious of these perceptions, beliefs and patterns, you will die the same way and about the same time that everyone else in your family who wasn't conscious has done. In this case, what you don't know will kill you. By the time you leave childhood, all of these perceptions, beliefs and patterns have already been planted in your unconscious. Fortunately, you will get many warnings before you get a fatal disease or have a fatal accident. The question is, will you heed these warnings, these calls to awaken, or will you return to your sleep until another warning signal wakes you up?

If you know what the patterns and perceptions are, it isn't hard to change them. However, some people may believe they are being disloyal to their family traditions if they decide to change their illness and death patterns. You also can perceive these illness and death patterns as part of the legacy curse of being born into your family, something over which you have no control. Some people decide to rebel against these patterns either by killing themselves, dying young or by trying to outlive their parents. In all cases, revenge becomes the motive, and the actual pattern still remains out of conscious awareness and is unchanged.

The only way out is through. That is, to break these patterns, you need to take responsibility for your life and your death. By discovering what your perceptions and fears of death are and where they came from, you can begin to make the process more conscious and therefore more changeable. Taking responsibility also means being conscious of those things you do that strengthen your life urges and weaken your death urges. This includes consciously choosing to eat foods that provide nourishment and strength for your body and avoiding junk foods or foods your body tells you are not good for you. It means exercising your body properly, as well as not putting undue psychological stress on your body. The latter may mean learning to play and relax, perhaps even developing spiritual and meditative practices that allow you to quiet your mind and relax.

Unraveling Your Family Death Patterns

The process of unraveling your family death patterns involves the following steps, which I will first list and then discuss individually.

1. Allow yourself to experience your fear of death.

2. Trace your family perceptions, beliefs and patterns about illness and death.

3. Develop a mind-body connection through the use of metaphysical causation.

4. Learn to use affirmations to clear negative thought patterns.

5. Develop a spiritual purification technique such as meditation or conscious breathing.

6. Develop good nutritional habits.

7. Develop a good body-work exercise program.

Experiencing Your Fear of Death

This seems like a tall order, but actually the fear of death is like any other fear. There are a number of ways to do this. I will mention a few examples. The first is one that I chose and it is through the use of a guided imagery. I was attending a workshop in 1970 during which the leader spoke about what he saw as the collective repression of fears of death. He offered to do a special evening session on this topic for people who were interested.

Five or six of us volunteered to experience a guided imagery process that he had designed to facilitate an experience of one's fear of death. The instructions were to imagine our own death, including how we thought we would die and under what circumstances, and then to experience the whole death process including seeing your obituary and attending your own funeral. My only experience with death

112

at that time was of my grandfather who died of cancer in a hospital at the same time I was in the same hospital having surgery.

So I began imagining myself lying in a hospital bed dying of cancer. Almost immediately, my breathing began to change and my body began to shake and vibrate in a convulsive manner. At first, I thought I was consciously creating these bodily reactions so I wasn't concerned. Then I tried to alter the reaction and found that all this was happening outside of my conscious control. That's when the fear really hit me. I thought, "I must be dying." I noticed that the more afraid I became, the more the shaking and convulsing increased. I also noticed that when I began to relax and accept that I couldn't control what was happening, the shaking would subside and a very peaceful feeling would ripple through my body. That seemed to be the only control I had left, to relax into the experience. The next twenty minutes or longer were filled with alternating periods of shaking and vibrating and then the peaceful feeling. Each time the peaceful feeling settled into my body, it seemed to be deeper and lasted longer before the shaking started again.

Finally, I sank into the most blissful, peaceful feeling I had ever experienced. I thought to myself, "This must be what death really is." Then I felt myself rising out of my body. I rose up to about four feet off the floor, and I could look down and still see my body lying on the floor. I was out of my body. I remember deciding that I didn't want to attend my funeral, although I could see my friends and family gathered. Then I began to move higher in the room, and finally I rose up through the roof of the building (we were on the top floor) and began to experience myself flying through space at an incredible rate of speed. All I could see were bright objects flashing by me as I flew out into deep space. These objects were bright and vibrant colors: red, orange, blue, green and violet.

I continued hurtling through space, but the blackness started to fade into grayness and then it began to get lighter and lighter until my whole visual field was filled with brilliant, golden, white light. I remember thinking that I must have gone back in time to the dawning of the universe. It was so brilliant and powerful and yet so peaceful that I was filled with tears of joy. I remained totally absorbed in the experience, and then gradually I felt myself coming back into my body and back into the room. Perhaps reentering my body startled me because I shuddered and then opened my eyes. Much to my surprise, several people were huddled around me with concerned looks on their faces. Later I learned that the facilitator of the exercise was quite concerned about me and had considered bringing me out of the experience. He was observing my alternating patterns of shaking and relaxing, and apparently at the moment when I experienced the final release and left my body, he observed that all the color drained out of my face, my lower jaw unhinged and my closed eyes rolled back into my head. I was totally unaware of any of these things and was surprised at his and other people's concern.

For several weeks after this experience, I struggled to understand what had happened. I seemingly had no framework to help me. Finally one day I told a friend about the experience, and as I finished telling him the details he looked at me in a strange way and said, "Have you read the *Tibetan Book of the Dead?*" I said that I hadn't and asked why he wanted to know. He then said, "What you described is written in that book and it recounts the experience of people who died and then came back to tell what it was like." Since then, I have read this book and others that tell about people who were clinically dead and then came back to describe their experience.

More importantly, the experience seemed to settle my fear of death. I will never forget the totally peaceful feeling I had. Since that time I have had several near-death experiences, one involving a boating accident, but even then my fear of death did not return. In fact, in each case I was able to keep thinking clearly and did not panic. I also spent twenty hours at the bedside of my wife, Barbara, just before she died of injuries from a skiing accident, and I was able to be calm and supportive. By now there are thousands or maybe even millions of people who have conquered their fear of death. Some of these people are now ministering to dying people and helping to shepherd them through this process.

I would recommend a guided imagery, such as the one I experienced, to be led by people who themselves have completed this or a similar process. If this experience feels like one you would like to have, you will need to find people trained to do this kind of work. If you do not know anyone, I would suggest contacting your minister or someone connected with Hospice, an organization that works with dying patients. Hospice often holds workshops and volunteer training programs in which they help potential volunteers deal with their fear of death.

Another way that I work with people on this issue is through breath work. One form of breath work, called "rebirthing," is designed to help people experience their fear of death by getting them to re-experience their own birth, the time when all of us were close to death and perhaps the original source of the fear of death. Again, if you choose this way to experience your fear of your death, you need to find a trained breath/body worker to help you with the process.

Although I know of people who have broken through this fear alone, perhaps through a vision quest or solo experience, or even through an unplanned near-death experience, you will have to decide how you will deal with your fear. I would suggest before you do anything like what was described above, you first get acquainted with your fear of death. Get to know it and begin to understand how it functions in your life. After you have done that, you will probably draw to you the necessary people or situations to help you resolve it.

There is a slogan that "the good die young." In part, I think it means that those people who have worked hard to break out of their other family patterns and *have not* dealt with their death patterns find these patterns finally consume them. If you bring to consciousness all the other blocks to growth and change, then all that may be left are your death patterns. If that is not also brought to full consciousness and integrated like everything else, then it could come like the Grim Reaper in the night to help manifest a death or near-death experience for you.

Tracing Your Family Death Patterns

We have covered this earlier in the chapter, so let me add only a few more suggestions here. Using the questions I suggested earlier, be sure to get information that spans at least three or four generations. These illness and death patterns run deep in families, and yet are often so obvious that an outsider or someone with an outside perspective can easily spot them. It is also important in your search for the patterns that you look for direct and indirect ways these patterns might be transmitted in your family.

One client told me almost proudly, "All the men in my family get arthritis of the spine. My great-grandfather and my grandfather and my father all have had it, and I have developed the early signs of it, too, in the past few years." It almost seemed like it was a requirement to join the men's club in that family. When we began to work with where this thought came from, we found that it was connected to holding in and holding on to feelings in his family. The men in that family had no permission to express their sadness or their joy, and so a hardness in the area of the spine behind the heart developed in each of these men. My client began to change this pattern and eventually threw away the pain pills he was taking. Now and again the symptoms would return as a reminder to him that he was blocking his feelings of sadness or joy.

CHAPTER THIRTEEN

Developing a Mind-Body Connection

*The great phase in man's
advancement is that in which he
passes from subconscious to
conscious control of his own mind
and body.*

—F.M. ALEXANDER

Most of us grew up being told that if we didn't put our boots on before going out in the winter snow, we would "catch a cold" or "get the flu." All these representations of how we get sick were taken literally as a belief that something from outside our body invades our body and makes us sick. This is the basis for the so-called "germ theory" of illness, which is the main medical theory in use in our culture. As this theory evolved over time, there have always been other theories to explain the causes of illnesses. Some are referred to as psychosomatic theories, or mind-body or metaphysical theories. A whole new field of medicine has developed to study body/mind connections. It is called psychoneuroimmunology.

The foundation of this new field is the belief that thoughts, beliefs and perceptions are what actually cause illness. Thoughts cause a biochemical reaction to occur in your body. The body listens to your thoughts and responds to every thought in some way. The body may tighten or relax, send signals to the various systems to release certain hormones or drugs into the bloodstream and in a million other unknown ways attempt to keep pace with your thoughts. We now know that our thoughts can directly affect our immune system and help us produce the antibodies necessary to deal with various foreign invaders and those that are there in your body most of the time.

Using this approach, it then becomes important to pay close attention to your thoughts and begin to link certain thought patterns with particular illnesses. This seems like a difficult task because you have so many thoughts and you may have trouble seeing how they could connect with an illness. Fortunately, there are some common sense rules to help you with this process:

1. Degenerative diseases such as cancer, arthritis, gallstones, ulcers and hypertension usually are caused by holding on to old resentments and hurts and letting things eat at you, or clinging to old ways.

2. Boils, burns, cuts, fevers, sores and inflammations are symptoms of angry thoughts that are being suppressed.

3. Tumors, cysts and growths also are connected to suppressing and holding on to old emotional hurts and shocks. They are bottled-up feelings from the past.

4. Strokes, arteriosclerosis and blood problems have to do with a lack of joy in your life and feeling clogged or bogged down by life.

5. Chronic pain of any kind has to do with guilt.

6. Breathing problems such as asthma and hay fever are connected to not having room to breathe, feeling smothered or not taking in much of life. They can also be related to uncried tears or unexpressed feelings.

7. Accidents represent rebellion against authority and anger at not being able to speak up or take care of yourself.

8. Eating problems and alcoholism are symptoms of self-hatred and self-rejection, thinking you are not good enough. They can also provide protection from having to be enough.

9. Back problems have three sets of thought patterns, depending on the location. Upper back problems have to do with a lack of emotional support, feeling unloved and holding back love. Middle back problems are related to guilt and wanting to get someone or something off your back or being burdened. Lower back problems relate to a lack of financial support and a fear of money.

There are several books by Louise Hay that contain specific thought patterns for almost every illness or body problem. Her small booklet, *Heal Your Body,* is a quick reference guide and a more extensive reference is in her book, *You Can Heal Your Life.* I would recommend either or both of these as basic references. I carry the small booklet with me all the time. They can be purchased from any new age bookstore or ordered directly from Louise Hay, 1242 Berkeley St., Santa Monica, CA 90404.

Using Affirmations

Once you begin to connect your negative thought patterns to certain illnesses or symptoms, then you will need to develop a new way of thinking to replace these old thought patterns. One such way is through the use of affirmations. Affirmations are highly charged, positive thoughts that will help surface and clear any unconscious negative thought pattern that runs counter to the affirmation. An affirmation is always written or stated in the present tense and without qualifiers. It can be stated from the first, second or third person perspective. ("I deserve love", "You [your name] deserve love" and "She/he deserves love.") I call any negative thought pattern "noise" or resistance. We have trained ourselves to perceive ourselves, other people and the world in certain ways that we call our "reality." What we don't realize is that we actually created that reality out of our perceptions and thoughts, and we can change that reality by changing our thoughts.

Awareness Activity

Try a short experiment with your thoughts. Take a pen or pencil and a piece of paper and write down every thought you have about yourself for the next five minutes. After you have finished, go back over your list. You may be surprised by how many thoughts you had. You may not have been able to record them all. Also notice how many thoughts about yourself are positive, neutral or negative. This can tell you much about the quality of your self-thoughts. If there were more neutral and negative thoughts then positive ones, you can look at what effect these thoughts might have on your body.

Affirmations help you to change these thoughts. There are a number of ways to work with affirmations:

1. to retrain the mind—repeat them as new thought patterns,
2. to help surface unconscious negative thought patterns, and
3. to clear and transform negative thought patterns.

By writing an affirmation or saying it aloud over and over, you can begin to retrain your mind to hold this new thought pattern. For example, someone who is too self–critical may write, "I now appreciate everything I do." Some people find that reminders such as posters or written messages in key places help keep their new thoughts in the foreground of their mind. Some people sing affirmations to themselves, while others repeat them aloud in front of a mirror.

The second way to work with affirmations is through the use of a response column immediately following the written affirmation to allow for any "noise" to surface. In this response column, you write down all thoughts which surface that run counter to the affirmation. You may in this way get more of the "noise" surfaced so you can clear it. For example, I might write, "I now appreciate everything I do," and suddenly a thought pops into my head. "I don't appreciate the way I get jealous sometimes." This noise can then be explored further to see what it is connected to.

The third way to use affirmations is for clearing the negative thoughts. Using the above example, I now have surfaced jealous feelings. To clear them, I need to find a way to reframe them into a new affirmation that is more positive. In this case, I might write, "I love my wife so much that I can now appreciate my jealous feelings toward her," or "My jealous feelings now remind me of how much I love my wife." In each case, I would wait for some further noise or negative counter-thoughts to surface. If none surfaced on repeated writings over several days, I would consider that old thought as cleared, and then further repeating and refining of the new thought will not be blocked by any more noise.

You can devise specific affirmations to change any family death patterns that you uncover. For example, if you uncover a cancer thought pattern related to holding on to deep hurt and long-standing resentment, you might write, "I now fully release my anger and resentment toward any and all people who may have hurt me in any way in the past. I now forgive them and release them to find their highest good in their own way. I now choose to fill my body with feelings of love and joy." You could then write or say these affirmations repeatedly (ten or twenty times) or use a response column to see if you can get to the surface any further negative thoughts that might be blocking these new thoughts. Then you can work with any negative thoughts until the old thoughts are cleared out, making room for the new ones. Whenever you thought about cancer, or something that reminded you of the old cancer thought pattern, you could then repeat the affirmation and check out whether any deeper resistance still existed.

If you actually have manifested an illness or symptom, you can use a general affirmation such as "I am now willing to release any thought patterns from my consciousness that have created this condition." Again using a response column, you can uncover any resistance you might have to this affirmation. If none appears, then proceed with a more specific affirmation related to your illness or symptom.

CHAPTER FOURTEEN

Spiritual Purification

> *Complete health and awakening*
> *are really the same.*
>
> —TARTHANG TULKU

Two of the most common tools for spiritual purification are meditation and prayer. Meditation and prayer, in their more pure forms, differ greatly because meditation is usually passive and prayer more active. The distinction breaks down, however, because some forms of meditation involve the use of active, verbal mantras or chanting and some forms of prayer involve a passive receptivity.

Certain forms of meditation seem particularly suited for changing your thoughts. One form is called Vipassana or Insight Meditation. It is from the Theravaden (Southern) Buddhist tradition and, in recent years, has become a popular form in the United States. Its popularity stems partly from its simplicity and the ease with which it can be taught. The practice, sometimes known as "sitting," requires that you sit with your back straight and watch your thoughts without being attached to them.

The suggested procedure is to be aware of your breath, by focusing on either the air as it passes in and out of your nostrils or the rising and falling of your abdomen. As you focus on your breath, you practice letting your thoughts float through your consciousness, without following them or doing anything with them. You can become a detached observer of your own thoughts and therefore do not have to get attached to them. Every time you start to get attached to a thought and want to follow it or do something with it, you simply return to focusing on your breathing. In this way, you learn non-attached awareness of your thoughts, which makes it easier to identify your thoughts and change them. In addition, the process of becoming less and less attached to the more "surface" thoughts seems to allow for a deeper or more spiritually evolved thought to come to the surface, producing insights.

Joseph Goldstein, one of the most well-known teachers of Vipassana Meditation in the U.S., wrote a book called *The Experience of Insight* (1976). He writes of this process, "It is important to make thoughts the object of mindfulness. If we remain unaware of thoughts as they arise, it is difficult to develop insight into their impersonal nature and into our own deep-rooted and subtle identification with the thought process." The practice of mindfulness can be extended beyond just sitting, as the goal of this form of meditation is to promote mindfulness in both your waking and sleeping activities. This helps people learn to be radically present and aware of everything in the moment without judgment or attachment. From this state, changing a thought or family pattern can be done in the blink of an eye. I hasten to add that however simple the process seems, it does take a long time of practice before one can be that radically present.

Awareness Activity:
Thought-Watching

You can practice and learn one of the basic meditative methods in a few minutes. Sit quietly for the next five minutes and practice just watching or observing your thoughts with your eyes either open or closed. Don't try to do anything with these thoughts; just observe them. You might see your thoughts going across a large screen or hear the thoughts being repeated in your mind. At the end of five minutes, take notice of the quality of these thoughts. What did you notice? Were your thoughts interesting or boring? Were they positive or negative? What did you like or dislike about your thoughts? Which thoughts did you like and dislike?

If you enjoyed the activity, you might experiment with "sitting" practice for fifteen to twenty minutes a day. Find a time when you will not be disturbed or interrupted, and practice staying focused on your breathing. At first, you may want to say the words "rising, falling" or "in, out" to help you keep focused. If a thought pulls you off your focus, objectively notice that it happened and then quickly return to focusing on your breath. You will find this difficult to do at first without criticizing yourself, so the less self-criticism you have, the easier it will become to stay focused.

This form of meditation also can be seen as a metaphor for the emerging definition of health. A person's state of health, physical or mental, can be determined by the amount of time and energy required to return to centeredness when one has been pulled off center by certain thoughts or external events. The quicker that a person can return to the centered state after being pulled off that state, the healthier we regard this person. We can tone our muscles and our thoughts in such a way that it makes it easier to return to centeredness. There is no way to really live in the world and expect to remain centered all the time. You may be driving to work, centered and relaxed, when a car suddenly pulls out in front of you or cuts you off. You have to react and temporarily go off center. Some people might allow that to upset their whole day, while others would return to being centered almost immediately. How well you have prepared your body/mind for this event through meditation or by practicing centering and relaxing will determine how quickly you can accomplish this.

Nutritional Awareness

It seems strange, but nutritional awareness is often one of the last areas to be awakened. Many people who have developed fine, personal growth skills are woefully lacking when it comes to nutritional awareness. Many people who know the connection between mind and body believe they can eat anything they want and believe they can use their thoughts to convert their junk-food diet into a good, balanced, nutritional one for their body. I'm sure that there are highly evolved people on the planet who, through years of practice, can accomplish this, but for most of us it is not possible.

At one time, all of us were able to read the signals from our body well enough to have it tell us which nutritional foods it wanted and needed, and which it didn't want or didn't need. Your ability to do that has been dulled by additives, preservatives and chemicals in processed foods, as well as by addictions to certain foods such as sugar, starch, salt or caffeine. Most of your addictions were learned from your family of origin. In addition, they taught you when to eat, how often to eat, how much to eat and how fast to eat. In some families, everyone eats on the run, while in others everyone is supposed to eat together at prescribed times. Meals in some families were tense and in others relaxed. What food and nutritional habits did you learn from your family of origin?

Some of us were taught specific rules of good nutrition, such as the famous "basic four" food groups that need to be present in your diet. In other families, no rules were taught. Your nutritional needs do change with age but they change also with your changes in consciousness.

Your body will have an allergic reaction to foods that have vibrational levels either too high or too low for it. As you clear out old, dysfunctional patterns or release stored feelings, your body will feel lighter and you will reach a higher vibrational level. You will need to change your diet to match this new level. If you do not change your diet, you will put undue pressure on your body. Also, if you don't follow good nutritional rules, your body will suffer even more than it did before your changes. The higher the vibrational level of your body, the more sensitive it becomes to foods, additives, preservatives, toxins, etc. Certain foods seem to have a higher vibration, while others have a lower vibration, so you will have to experiment until you find the foods that fit the current vibrational level of your body.

Before you can safely experiment, you should know some basic facts about food, nutrition and digestion. I recommend that you seek a good nutritionist to help educate you and/or read some good books on the subject. *Diet and Nutrition* (1978) by Dr. Randolph Ballentine is an excellent reference. You can also check at your local health food store and often find some good free literature and other suggested reading.

The following are some of the basic nutritional facts you will need to know:

1. Foods may be classified as acid or alkaline. A balanced diet should have no more than twenty percent acid-forming foods. Consult a nutritional table to determine which foods are acid or alkaline.

2. In the summer, you should eat eighty percent raw food. In the winter, this can be reduced to fifty percent.

3. Phase out dairy products, especially in combination with sweets. They clog your system and result in poor digestion. Meats are also very hard to digest and should be eaten only in small quantities.

4. Omit all processed and refined foods. They have little or no nutritional value.

5. Do not drink liquids with your meals. It slows down digestion. Liquids should be drunk at least one-half hour before a meal and not right after a meal. Wait several hours.

6. Avoid combining foods as much as possible. For example, don't eat proteins and carbohydrates together, or fats and proteins, sugars and proteins, acids and proteins, or acids and starches.

7. Don't eat fruits and vegetables at the same meal.

8. Don't ever eat when feverish, anxious, in pain, angry, overheated or chilled.

9. Use only natural sweeteners such as raw honey, maple syrup or fructose. Refined sugars are too quickly metabolized to have any nutritional benefit. They also overtax the pancreas and cause blood sugar reactions.

10. Don't cook with grease (lard, butter or hardened vegetable oil).

11. Eliminate salt; it overtaxes the heart, kidneys, bladder, circulatory system and nervous system.

12. Always eat melons by themselves; also eat avocados alone and drink milk alone.

Using these basic facts and any other reliable information you find on nutrition, you can begin to experiment to find out which foods your body is allergic to and which foods match your body's vibration. Check out only those foods you suspect. Eat the food by itself and notice any reactions in your body. Allergic symptoms might include increased mucus in nose or throat, sneezing, indigestion, gas, sluggishness, dizziness, bad taste in your mouth in the morning and a prolonged feeling of fullness in the stomach.

Another method now being used to check on nutritional balances is called applied kinesiology. A person trained in this approach can check for instant reactions to any food or vitamin-mineral supplement. You sit with your back straight and with your non-dominant hand in your lap (left, if you're right-handed, right, if you're left-handed) with the palm open and facing upward. Your dominant arm is held straight ahead, shoulder height, with the palm down. The kinesiologist places a bit of the food to be tested in your non-dominant palm and then applies downward pressure to the dominant, outstretched arm. If the body registers an allergic reaction, the arm will weaken and can be pushed down. If the food is good for your body, the arm will remain strong when pushed on. In this way, all foods and supplements can be checked on, as well as jewelry or watches. Certain metals also can weaken the body.

Food allergies can be cleared up through proper diet (by avoiding the allergin), proper food combinations, vitamin-mineral supplements and proper digestion. Sometimes enemas and colonics may be used to flush out putrefied material from the intestines in order to allow for proper digestion to develop.

Finally, daily skin brushing is recommended to help your skin stay vital and help your body eliminate toxins. Brushing the skin with a long-handled, natural vegetable bristle brush for four or five minutes once or twice a day cleanses the lymphatic system. (These brushes can usually be found in a natural food store.)

Depending on the level of the imbalance, it can take six months or more to bring your whole system back into balance. As your body detoxifies, it can only eliminate toxins at a certain rate. If toxins are released into the bloodstream too fast, a cleansing reaction will not occur. Fasting is not usually recommended in this process because it usually causes toxins to be released into the bloodstream faster than the body can eliminate them.

The results of good nutritional balance in the body usually make the effort worthwhile. However, the thought patterns imbedded in food tissues are very resistant to change, and you will need self-discipline, patience and support. When I began this kind of a program, all sorts of food cravings and obsessional thoughts about food surfaced for me. Most of us are nutritionally ignorant as well, so it requires hard work to develop good nutritional habits.

Developing A Body Work/Exercise Program

We have learned through the work of Dr. Wil Penfield and others that memories of old patterns are stored in parts of our brain. We have also realized that these old memories and suppressed feelings are stored in the nerve endings located in the muscles and connective tissues of the body. Certain types of body work, such as Rolfing or acupressure, can cause these messages to be released from the muscles and connective tissues. Rolfing and other similar types of deep tissue manipulation do seem to cause stored emotional messages to be released so they can be brought into consciousness.

127

The various forms of yoga can also be used to help the body release stored-up psychological material, including the fear of death. Yoga is the science of union with the Divine and with Truth. It is a complete mind/body/spirit practice, so it can offer many more benefits than just exercising. The regular practice of yoga helps to bring your metabolic system into balance with the rest of you. In this way, you can metabolize your food correctly and gain the maximum nutritional value from what you eat, provided you also use sound nutritional practices like those described above. Patanjali, the father of modern yoga, described the benefits of yoga as: 1) the natural regulation of the nervous system, 2) a mental discipline, 3) body cleansing, 4) improved flexibility, 5) improved powers of concentration, 6) improved ability to contemplate, 7) increased consciousness and 8) the development of an inner state of tranquility.

Yoga can be supplemented easily by aerobic exercises such as cycling, skiing, tennis, jogging and swimming. Even those forms of exercise often quiet the mind and have spiritual value as well. For example, tennis for me is a game that helps me orient myself in the here and now. While playing tennis, I can easily notice where I leave this present focus. If I am late in hitting the ball, it is always because I have fallen back into the past. I may be still thinking about the last shot I missed or made, or even thinking about things I was doing just before starting the tennis match. If I notice I am ahead of the ball and hitting it long, it is because my thoughts are drifting into the future, anticipating something, instead of staying in the present. Then when I am hitting the ball accurately, I know that I am keeping focused on the here and now. The bodily feeling I have in that state is very similar to the one I have when I am meditating and I drop into pure awareness without thought. In that state, my body knows exactly what to do and I don't need to think about it. In fact, when I consciously try to think about what to do, I almost automatically leave the here and now, and the ball sails out of the court!

PART II

THE RECOVERY OF YOUR TRUE SELF

He that falls in love with himself
will have no rivals.

—BENJAMIN FRANKLIN

Introduction

In Chapter 2, "The Process of Recovery of Our True Self" was introduced and explained briefly. Part I of the book (Chapters 1 through 14) covered Steps 1–3 of that process, namely, becoming aware of our unresolved issues from childhood and our family patterns that show up in our present relationships. Part II will cover the rest of the steps in the Process of Recovery of Our True Self (Chapters 15 through 20) as well as my own story.

Since this part of the book is designed to help you recover your true self, let's look at that goal more closely. Some would say if children were allowed to develop their true self during childhood, they would later become martyrs because they would refuse to adapt to society's norms. Parents try to get their children to learn to adapt as early as possible so that they learn to get along with authority figures and won't suffer any abuse later on at school or on the job. Parents also give their children double messages about this: "Grow up and be your own person; be what others want you to be in order to get along in the world."

While children who adapt and conform to adult standards do not cause parents or their teachers any trouble, very often they are cut off from their own natural emotions of anger, joy, sadness, excitement or fear. They replace these natural feelings with unnatural emotions of guilt, resentment, envy, anxiety, self-pity and depression. Children who have been treated with respect, understanding and love during childhood are able to survive childhood with their natural emotions intact. As adults, these people are better able to see through hypocrisy and therefore are better able to take care of themselves. They are not as easily taken in by the illusions and deceptions of people and society. These people do not become martyrs to society but usually lead happy and productive lives that allow them to be in the world, but not of the world.

People who have learned respect by being respected can give respect to others without feeling compliant. People who have been cared for will care for others who are weaker than themselves. People who have been loved for who they are become tolerant, understanding and loving toward others. People who have learned to develop their own values and ideals, allow others to do the same. In short, these people make good citizens in a democracy where everyone is free to pursue his or her own life as long as it doesn't interfere with the same rights of others.

For an adult who is trying to recover what was lost during early childhood, the process is not an easy one. Above all, it takes spiritual courage to recover this vital life force within you. It also requires some safety and support. Very few people can venture into the unknown realms of their depths to find and reclaim their lost parts without some support from a group of friends and fellow venturers and/or from an intimate partner in a committed relationship. Many of the beginning steps in the process of becoming aware of your family patterns and what needs fixing can be taken alone or at times with others. The rest of the process of recovery of your true self is best done with others in some sort of ongoing support or therapy group or with your willing partner. Without this kind of support, the process is much more difficult and maybe impossible for most human beings.

I am reminded of the story of the third voyage of Columbus to the New World. After his first two voyages, he became a hero and his findings helped to reshape the world view of all the great thinkers of his time. On his third voyage, he was blown off course and sailed to the mouth of the Orinoco River in South America. When he was confronted by the downward-flowing turbulence of this river, he became frightened. He suddenly saw that his theories might have been wrong.

He thought this water was running downhill from a holy mountain containing the Garden of Eden and all its forbidden secrets. He could not explore any further and fled back home instead. He feared that the round-world theory that he had proclaimed would now have to be changed. With the image of the holy mountain filling his senses, Columbus visualized the earth on one side as shaped like a pear. So rather than destroy the maps and theories of the old world and risk his reputation, he hesitated and turned back.

This is a reminder to you as you destroy the maps and patterns set forth for you by your family of origin. Even though the possibility of a paradise exists beyond these limitations, you may hesitate and seek to return to the safety and security of the familiar. You may come to the edges of your known world and become afraid that you can't reach the other side and that you will fall into the chasm and be lost forever, no longer able to climb back to the safety of the old ways or able to find your way to the light of the new world. These are the fears you must confront with spiritual courage to carry you forward to reach your goals.

CHAPTER FIFTEEN

Expressing Repressed Feelings

We all start out perfect. You begin to see that people become twisted when their natural emotions are suppressed.

—ELIZABETH KÜBLER-ROSS
The Function of Feeling

The Function of Feeling

Feelings, as a word for emotions, sympathies and susceptibilities, was first used in English in 1771. (Hillman 1979) Today in our modern world where academic values prevail, there doesn't seem to be much room for feelings. There is a collective repression of the feeling side of the personality, leaving most of us with a sense of loss. Loss seems to be the main thought we have when we think of our feelings. We are at a loss, not knowing how or what to feel. We don't know where to feel, why to feel or even if we should feel at all. This has a crippling effect on our ability to form solid values, ideals and beliefs and to make good decisions. Our schools have failed to teach us anything about how our feelings function. Rousseau once said: "He among us who can best carry the joys and sorrows of life, in my opinion is the best educated." He would not want to look among the holders of academic degrees to find such a person today.

So we find ourselves even unsure of the actual function of feelings in our lives. Their main function is to help us make distinctions between and among various preferences. We ask: "What do you feel like doing?" or we say, "That doesn't feel good to me and this feels better." If you don't know your feelings or are cut off from them, you

132

often don't know what you want. You don't know how to choose or decide the important questions in your life. What most people do is let other people decide for them or go along with what is expedient.

You need to educate yourself about your feelings if you are going to be free to form your own values, ideals and choices. One of the first lessons is to understand what your natural feelings are and what the function of each feeling is. Below is a list of basic feelings and their specific function:

1. *Anger*—A natural response we make that lets us know that a want or need is not being met or hasn't been met in the past. *Rage, frustration, hatred* and *boredom* are words that represent degrees of anger.

2. *Fear*—A natural response to perceived physical or emotional danger. *Panic, terror* or *anxiety* represent degrees of fear.

3. *Sadness*—A natural response to the perceived loss of a person, valued possession, relationship or something we want. *Grief, hurt* and *loneliness* are words to represent degrees of sadness.

4. *Excited*—A natural response to the anticipation of something good happening. Other feeling words that relate to being excited are *eager* and *hopeful*.

5. *Happy or Joyful*—A natural response to getting something you want or need. Also could be a response to doing something you wanted to do. Other related feeling words are *glad, pleased* or *ecstatic*.

Most of these natural feelings were suppressed and denied during childhood so you cannot utilize them effectively in making decisions. Instead, you use substitute feelings like guilt, resentment, envy, jealousy and depression to make your decisions. According to Alice Miller (1983) in her book *For Your Own Good,* you stay stuck in infancy because you were:

1. hurt as a small child, without anyone noticing your hurt,
2. told not to be angry at being hurt,
3. forced to show gratitude toward those who hurt you because they had good intentions (they didn't mean to hurt you),
4. told to forget everything that happened, and
5. shown how to discharge the stored-up anger onto others in adulthood or were shown how to direct it against yourself.

She adds that, "The greatest cruelty that can be inflicted on children is to refuse to let them express their anger and suffering except at the risk of losing their parents' love and affection." (p. 106) For example, parents do not understand how to handle temper tantrums in children. The child is using the tantrum to discharge accumulated tension and frustration. Once the tantrum is over, the child feels peaceful inside. He or she is ready to forgive and be forgiven. However, parents find it difficult to forgive and forget. They are afraid this will only encourage more temper tantrums. What a child needs is a warm hug and some reassurance that he or she is still loved and cherished. If parents punish or humiliate the child, this only sets the stage for another build-up of tension that will need to be discharged. If parents are able to empathize with their children when they are feeling hurt, angry, defenseless or humiliated, it is like looking themselves in the mirror and seeing the hurt, anger, fear and suffering of their own childhood. Many parents cannot bear to look at all their childhood pain, so they do something to ward it off out of the fear of being consumed by the feelings.

Those parents who have mourned their childhood losses and sufferings are able to accept and empathize with their children. These people have learned more about feelings and human behavior than they ever could from a book. Our children are our ultimate teachers. They present us with everything that we think we have successfully hidden from the world and from ourselves. Maybe someday we will begin to regard our children not as objects to manipulate and control but loving messengers from a world we once knew, but have long since forgotten. These messengers can reveal the secrets of life to us and can tell us more about our own lives than our parents were ever able to.

Other feelings are actually too intense for many young children to feel. Deep sadness is much too painful for young children. Deep sadness would have to include a full recognition that the world is not all that one had imagined. Instead of feeling this deep sadness, children will become extra active and lively or they may get angry. Also, parents may have trouble witnessing a child who is trying to express sadness, and some parents attempt to interrupt the child's valiant efforts to confront sadness by encouraging him/her to smile and play some game. To the child this may mean that being sad is another way of displeasing his or her parents.

Ways to Elicit Repressed Feelings

We all left childhood with some of our natural feelings suppressed or repressed. Frequently, we are totally cut off from these feelings and we have to find some way to make contact with old feelings. We may cry when we hear a sad story or see a sad movie. These are some of our uncried tears from childhood, but we usually feel embarrassed about our tears and choke them off again. What you need to do at those times is go back to where the tears came from and connect with the original hurt or sadness or rejection you felt at that time. If you can relive that moment and fully express the feelings, then you can begin to release the stored energy that was bottled up in your body/ mind at the time. Most people are so afraid of these feelings that their natural tendency is to shut them off when they come up. To do emotional release work, you have to avoid that tendency and let the feelings surface, as well as try to connect the feelings with specific childhood experiences. Sometimes you cannot connect the feelings with a specific childhood incident, so in those cases all that is necessary is to experience the feelings as fully as possible and know that healing is taking place.

Anger Work

Anger is the most common childhood feeling that was suppressed. When anger is expressed naturally, it lasts ten to fifteen seconds and then it is over. When suppressed anger comes out, it usually lasts five to ten minutes, but then it is also over. When people feel safe to express their suppressed anger fully, it often comes out as a homicidal rage and, at that moment, they could kill, but it, too, passes quickly in five to ten minutes. Afterward, these people wouldn't harm a fly and they feel the freedom that this release brings. If people can be assisted by others who are not scared of these intense feelings, then they will go through the experience completely and never have to do that again. Some people scare themselves midway through the experience and try to close down the feelings. This is harmful. These people need lots of encouragement and support to complete the expression of their suppressed rage.

When people can blow up in this way, they stop blowing up inside themselves, stop allowing the anger to eat away at them or stop blowing up at others. They become truly peaceful. When people express suppressed sadness or anger in a group setting, frequently there

135

is a ripple effect where one person's work will trigger feelings for others. After each time a person expresses suppressed feelings, time should be allotted for others to share their feelings, which often helps them to get their feelings out. As mentioned earlier in the book, anger work often requires beating a pillow or bed with a tennis racquet or rolled-up towel. It may also require someone to be held down by others to get to the rage. Some people need to kick or pound pillows to get the anger out. Often when anger or rage is expressed fully, it is followed by sadness and grief, which is very healing. We need to mourn all this and then let it go.

Open-Ended Sentences

The following list of open-ended sentences can be used to elicit suppressed feelings. You can either read them aloud, have someone else read them to you (changing the pronoun to "you") or write out your answers (write the first thing that comes to you). It also is good to repeat each sentence to get to deeper responses.

When I wake up in the morning . . .
Ever since I was a child . . .
My Mother always . . .
My Mother never . . .
My Mother seemed to expect . . .
That made me feel . . .
And it also made me feel . . .
All my life . . .
Why do I always . . .
Right now I am feeling . . .
Sometimes I want to cry out . . .
My Father always . . .
My Father never . . .
My Father seemed to expect . . .
That made me feel . . .
And it also made me feel . . .
If I make a mistake . . .
When my parents saw me make a mistake . . .
If I ever let out my anger . . .
I feel sad that . . .

It scares me to . . .
I resent . . .
I dread . . .
Whenever I try . . .
When I look at my body . . .
I am a person who . . .
Why do people try to . . .
When people look at me . . .

If any of these items seems to elicit strong feelings, then follow the feelings back to some childhood incident. Tell or write the incident in present tense, as if it were happening now, and let the feelings emerge. If you are working with a partner, have your partner act as a cheerleader to elicit the full expression of the feelings, such as "Tell me more about how you feel," "Let it all come up" or "Don't hold back."

Breath-Work

Simple, connected breathing can bring suppressed hurt and sad feelings to the surface and allow them to be released quickly and easily. The connected breathing technique I use for this is to have the person connect the inhale and the exhale with no pause between. I ask them to visualize a circle, with the inhale being half and the exhale the other half. I ask them to breathe through their nose or their mouth and pull the air in on the inhale and let it go on the exhale.

There is a built-in release mechanism on the exhale, and usually within fifteen to twenty minutes of this kind of breathing, feelings will begin to surface for the person. The main thing, even though they may want to cry, is to keep them in their breathing rhythm, which will allow the release to occur. They may also start to shake or vibrate and tingle as their feelings are released from the body.

Another powerful tool to use in conjunction with the connected breathing is to ask them to locate the feeling in their body. Sadness is often located in the chest or sometimes the face or throat. After they locate the feeling, ask them to intensify the feeling for a short time and then have them begin to spread the feeling throughout their body. Have them feel it spreading out from the place where they first located it until their whole body is filled with the feeling. This full-body experience of the feeling seems to release it and diffuse it until it is gone. Once the feeling is experienced throughout the body, it loses its hold on the body and the mind. People no longer fear the feeling when it is expressed this way. Afterward, they usually feel very relaxed and peaceful.

Body-Work

Another process that produces a full release involves some body work. By using certain stress postures, you can loosen suppressed feelings that are stored in the muscles of your body. While standing with feet shoulder–width apart and feet turned in slightly, you can bend backwards with your closed hands resting on the top of your buttocks in the back. Hold that posture until shaking and vibrating starts in your abdomen, pelvis or thighs. Then reverse it by bending forward at the waist, with your feet at shoulder width and turned inward. This helps put stress on the calf muscles, which is a favorite storage area for anger. The abdomen, pelvis and thighs often store fear, hurt and sadness as well as repressed sexual feelings. These postures will bring a release of these feelings and may help you connect them to childhood experiences.

Yoga can be used in this way as well. Certain yoga postures allow the body to release suppressed emotions naturally. Sometimes when people are expressing anger or sadness, they will go into spontaneous yoga postures that utilize expression of these feelings. Massage, Rolfing, acupressure and other forms of body work are also useful to help uncover and release stored emotional content from the body.

In the next chapter, we will look at a structured method for uncovering and releasing unexpressed feelings from childhood. In this method, you will be asked to write about your negative experiences with your mother and your father and then use that written material to help you elicit your suppressed feelings.

CHAPTER SIXTEEN

The Prosecution of Your Parents

Almost no child has the parents he or she deserves.

—BOB HOFFMAN

The Prosecution of Your Parents

The next step in the process of recovery of your true self is a written and verbal prosecution of each of your parents. (Hoffman 1976) The goal of this step is to finally purge all the negative feelings that you are aware of and that still remain unexpressed toward each parent. This step asks you to recall and relive the memory of the pain, hurt and anger for the narcissistic wounds and wrongs you suffered as a result of what your parents said, did or didn't say or didn't do to you. By writing these memories, you will help clear the negative effects these feelings are having on you. Remember that they are only feelings and that no matter how intensely you feel them now, they cannot harm you. What can harm you is not expressing these feelings, allowing them to cause more tension and dis-ease in the body.

Taking each parent, step-parent or other people instrumental in your childhood development, begin by making a list of his or her traits, moods and feelings that you felt had some negative effects on you. Also, it is important to include the feelings you experienced but probably never expressed. Even if you cannot remember how you felt, imagine yourself or someone else experiencing the particular incident and ask, "How would anyone feel who had that happen to them? Would they feel afraid, hurt, angry, sad, happy or excited?" Use the following questions to organize your thoughts, listing examples under each question. The best way to write this is to blame everything bad that ever happened to you on the way your mother or father treated you as a child. Using this approach, don't offer excuses for their behavior. Also, don't try to blame yourself in any way. (Ex: "I was a lot of trouble for them.") For the purposes of this activity, try to blame one hundred percent of your problems on your parents and the ways they treated you or didn't treat you as a child. The prosecutor has to present the strongest case possible in order to find them guilty. In this way, you can fully purge all the negativity stored in your body and break the lock that these unexpressed feelings have had on your growth. Start this process with the prosecution of your mother.

The Prosecution of Mother

Were you wanted by your mother? Were you planned for or were you an "accident"? Were you the sex your mother wanted you to be? Did your mother love you for who you are or did she want you to be a certain way? Were your needs ignored or were you treated like a burden for your mother? How did she show love to you? Was she too busy to show attention to you? How did your mother teach you to relate to your brothers and sisters?

What was your first day of school like? Did your mother prepare you for this or did she sort of dump you there? Did you feel abandoned by her? Did she show she really cared about what you were doing in school? How did she respond when you brought home your treasured school project? Later, how did she deal with your report cards? Was she indifferent to your progress? Did she criticize or praise your progress? What expectations did she have for you? Did she come to school on parents' day?

How did your mother handle special days like your birthday, Christmas and other holidays? Were these festive and joyous occasions or were they a burden for her? Was your birthday party for you or for her? Or did she totally ignore your birthday? How did she respond to the gifts you gave her?

How did your mother discipline you? Did she smack you for doing things that bothered her? Or did she ignore you and never give you any clear guidelines for how she wanted you to behave? Did she give you the silent treatment or withdraw her love to show disapproval or displeasure? Did she leave discipline for your father? Was she fair in her punishment of you? Did she see you as sinful when you misbehaved? Did she ever admit that she was wrong in what she said or did? Did she make you feel unloved when she punished you? How did your mother handle your need for independence? Did she make you dependent on her and try to hold on to you, or did she push you out of the nest too soon, without giving you good information and guidance? Did she encourage you to try new things and explore your world, or did she discourage your efforts? What kind of information did she give you about living in the world? Did she give you her fears? Did she set rules without giving you reasons for having the rules? How did she respond to your questions or requests for information on how to grow up?

How did your mother handle your illnesses? Did she make you feel guilty for getting sick and causing her problems? Did she teach you that getting sick was the only way to get sympathetic attention from her? Did she know how to deal with your illnesses or did she get confused and helpless?

What was your mother's attitude toward your father? Did she respect and understand him? Did she hold him up as a worthy example to emulate or did she run him down, criticizing and emasculating him? Did she manipulate your father? Was she an equal with him or did she act like a frightened victim, obediently taking orders? What example did she set for you?

How did your mother treat your friends? Was she jealous of anyone who took you away from her or did she push you away, forcing other people on you to keep you occupied? Did she try to pick your friends for you? Did she undermine your confidence in choosing friends by criticizing your choices? Did she try to prejudice you against certain groups of people?

Did your mother laugh and have fun? Was she able to see the funny side of herself as well as others, or was she serious and humorless? Was she able to enjoy life and see the lighter side of life's inevitable problems and perplexities?

What kind of sex education did your mother provide? Did she give you good information about sexuality or did she ignore the subject? Did she attempt to impose her standards on you or did she allow you freedom to choose your standards?

This process of writing out the memories of negative experiences you had with your mother and the emotions attached to them will help you to see the negative effect your mother really had on you. This written litany serves as preparation for the next step in your "purging process": the verbal outpouring of negative feelings toward your mother.

The Verbal Prosecution

This part of the process helps you mobilize your inner resources to move out of a victim position that may have been evident in your written prosecution of your mother. This step requires that you get enraged and hateful toward your mother, telling her how angry you are at her for what she did or didn't do to you. This usually does not have to be done directly with your mother, but can be done by imagining your mother's face on a pillow and yelling and pounding that pillow. Or you can imagine your mother's face on another person who can act out your mother's part and make it more real. Most people are able to purge themselves of their unexpressed negative feelings in these ways. It is helpful to have four or five people present to help facilitate the process. The prosecutor should wear loose, comfortable clothing to permit free movement.

This activity is very frightening for some people, and they need considerable support and nudging from trusted friends and loved ones to complete this step. If they get stuck, several people may have to model how to do it, or speak for the person for a while to help give them the courage to go through with it. It is important that the prosecutor use street language and curse words because of their shock value. It is also useful if the session can be videotaped or audiotaped with someone assigned to watch for body movements that indicate stuck places. By going over the session at a later time, the prosecutor can learn more about this part of the process. Sometimes this step in the process has to be repeated a number of times before a complete purging is experienced. What happens to people when they really experience their own negativity is that they are shocked at how much like their negative mother they actually are. They begin to see how much they have been cut off from that part of themselves.

If the prosecutor can express his or her full rage with a total lack of restraint and an animal-like fury, this negativity can be purged in ten to fifteen minutes. However, people should be encouraged to continue until *they* feel all their negative energy is spent. This can take an hour or more for some people. It is important that people experience at least a partial completion of this step. Because you don't want to have to hold back in any way, it may be necessary to alert neighbors or find a place where no one can hear you scream, yell, pound, curse, cry or thump. It is important that the session continue until the prosecutor has broken through to their gut-level anger.

At a deep level, everyone has narcissistic wounds that they received at the hands of their mother during childhood. We are all very angry at not being taken seriously, at not being respected and mirrored for who we were and at not being treated the way we hoped they would treat us. Often when this anger is completely purged, you are left with a deep sadness and grief over losing your true self in the process of growing up, perhaps knowing that your childhood is irretrievably lost. There is no way to return to the innocence and bliss you experienced as a child, before you were wounded. You can only heal your wounds and move on. For most of us, it means looking at life the way it really is, not the way we had hoped or wished it would be. This is a sobering experience indeed, one that we are often afraid to face. When you do face yourself and the reality of your life, you can accept it with mourning. People who have mourned their loss in this way are able to understand much more about the dynamics of the human psyche than they could have ever learned by reading books.

Here is an example of this purging process. John was a loner and had tried to avoid his mother as much as possible while he was growing up. The written account of his experiences with his mother was filled with references to not being seen and feeling as though he was invisible to his mother. He frequently felt dead inside and suffered from acute depression from time to time. Several incidents from his negative emotional journal are worth noting.

> I recall being dropped on my head by my mother when I was about two. I don't remember how it happened, but she was carrying me and I wanted to get down. I guess I squirmed out of her arms and she dropped me on my head. I was knocked out and scared and hurt. When I regained consciousness, she screamed at me for doing something wrong. I even wished I had died so as not to hear her screaming at me.
>
> Once when I was about eight, on a family vacation we all were staying in one motel room and I had a bad cold. I couldn't

help it but I coughed during the night. My mother said if I coughed one more time she would make me sleep in the car. Even though I tried not to, I coughed again and she made me sleep in the car. It was March and very cold; she wouldn't let me take a blanket with me because they didn't want to be cold. I ended up getting really sick from this and she said I ruined the family's vacation. I often thought I would have been better off had I died from that.

When John tried to express his rage verbally, he had a lot of trouble. He said, "I feel angry and resentful toward my mother, but when I try to express it, I tend to excuse her behavior and blame it on myself. I say, 'If only I had . . . ,' or 'Why didn't I . . . ,' and it takes her off the hook." When someone else goaded him by acting like his mother, he began to open up. This woman said, "Johnny, you just need to behave yourself and do as I tell you and everything will be fine. I will tell you everything you need to know. Don't think for yourself, you are too stupid anyway to do it right. Here, I will show you how."

Slowly, John began to direct his anger at this person:

I hate you, you fucking bitch. You made me afraid of everything. Why the hell didn't you teach me how to get along in this world? You pretended to know it all and you didn't know shit. You fucked me over royally and then shit all over me. I hate you for all the bullshit you threw at me. I never got a straight answer in my life from you. Nothing but bullshit. You lied to me about everything. You lied to me about love, you lied to me about people, and I am so sick and tired of your bullshit I could puke all over you. [John was then given a tennis racquet and a large pillow to pound on.] I hate you. I want to smash you to pieces for what you did and didn't do. [John hit the pillow violently, screaming and yelling his words.] I hate you, I hate you. Die, you bitch!

After about ten minutes of pounding the pillow and yelling, John collapsed in a sweat, breathing rapidly. His whole body shook and vibrated. All he could say was, "Wow! I did it." This process must also be completed with your father. You must purge all the negative feelings you have toward your father using the same procedure as the one you used to deal with your feelings toward your mother. Frequently, dealing with fathers is more difficult because they were not there, and their crimes were ones of omission and not so much of commission.

That is why it is good to prepare for dealing with your father by first dealing with your mother. One female client, Jan, said, "My father was never home. He seemed to drop in and sleep there, but he was rarely involved in the daily happenings of our home. Mother did all that and I guess she shielded him from any of the problems we were having. Consequently, I never got to know the man called my father. He was almost a stranger to me."

The Prosecution of Father

Using the same approach you used with your mother, describe your relationship with your father while you were growing up. Again, blame one hundred percent of your problems as an adult on the ways your father treated you or didn't treat you as a child. Be sure to include all of your feelings toward your father as you recall incidents from your childhood. Use the following questions to guide you in writing the prosecution of your father.

What kind of father did you have? Was he available to you or did he turn over the job of raising you to your mother? How did he feel about your birth? Did he look forward to your coming into the family or did he see you as an unwanted burden? Were you the sex your father wanted or did you disappoint him? If you were his son, did he expect you to fulfill all of his unfulfilled ambitions or was he jealous of you, teaching you never to be better than him in any way? If you were his daughter, how did he deal with you? Did he ignore you or did he try to turn you into a substitute son? What did your father teach you by example about men? Was he cold and distant, or weak and immature, needing constant attention?

How did your father relate to you when you were an infant? Did he play with you gladly, or grudgingly out of guilt? Was he a fair–weather father who was only interested in you when you were happy or if you didn't ask for anything in return? Later, did he brush you off with a head pat or an angry rebuke for bothering him? Did he hold you and give you time, or did he retreat by taking a nap or a drink or by burying himself in his newspaper or television programs?

How did your father wield his power in your home? Was he a tyrant, always angrily insisting on getting his own way, or was he a weakling who gave in to everyone? Did he teach you to be weak in this way? Did your father allow your mother to dominate him?

Was he frequently inconsistent in his love and affection for you?

145

Did you sometimes think he wished you weren't around or that you were just another mouth to feed? Did he praise your accomplishments and correct your errors? Did you get mostly negative attention from him and therefore still find yourself setting it up to get negative attention from other men? What kind of discipline did your father use on you? Was he fair or was he cruel, or did he just ignore you, refusing to get involved in disciplining you?

How did your father handle money with you? Was he generous with you or did he make you beg for money every time you wanted to buy something for yourself? Did he try to buy your love with presents that were really bribes or guilt offerings? Did he teach you to manage money through an allowance and paid household chores? Did he inform you of the family's financial status or keep you in the dark about this? How did he react to gifts you gave him? Was he unresponsive or unhappy with the gifts you bought him?

How did your father react to your school work? Did he have impossible expectations for you to meet or did he ignore your school accomplishments? Did he attend school activities to watch you perform or was he always too busy? Did he insist that you live up to his expectations of you? Did he withdraw his love if you failed to do so?

How did your father handle his job? Was he a compulsive workaholic so you hardly ever saw him, or was he shiftless and unreliable, causing financial burdens for you and the family? Did he have poor health or die during your childhood, thus deserting you and the family?

How did he handle your sex education? Did he tell off-color jokes about sex or did he ignore your sexual development? What were his acts of omission? What did he fail to provide for you?

When the prosecution of both parents is complete, many people feel exhausted and exhilarated. They often feel strong, alert and relaxed in their body as well. From this state of relaxed openness, they are then able to make the abrupt shift from prosecutor to defense counsel for their mother and father. The next chapter will deal with the defense of mother and father.

The Defense of Your Parents

Everyone is guilty and no one is to blame.
—BOB HOFFMAN

After the written and verbal prosecution of your parents, during which you were able to purge yourself of all unexpressed negative feelings, you now may be ready to engage in a written and verbal defense of your parents. It is essential for you to experience your parents as real people who were also victims of unhealed narcissistic wounds from their own childhood. This enables you to transcend the blame and negativity and reach a new level of understanding. Again, I caution you against doing this before you have completely cleared out the negativity stored in your body. If you get stuck anywhere in the defense part of the process, go back to the prosecution stage and do further work there before continuing.

The defense of your parents can lead you to absolve them and you of any karmic ties you may have had. This also helps prevent these karmic patterns from being passed on to your children. If you already have children, it will permit any karmic patterns you have with them to be broken as well. So by doing this work, you are influencing your family patterns for at least three generations and maybe more. Once you fully understand the damage you have experienced from your parents, you can more fully understand the damage you have done or may be doing to your own children.

There are three distinct steps in the defense of each parent. The first step involves a dialogue with witnesses to defend each parent. Step two then involves your imagined testimony by each parent about their own childhood, while step three includes your trial summary.

These three steps can be written, or they can be acted out with a group of people, having them help by playing the appropriate roles. Also, you can use empty chairs and pillows to dialogue with these witnesses. Usually some combination is necessary to work out the defense of each parent.

In step one, the key witnesses should be either your parents as children or their parents. Other witnesses may be used to fit each situation. For example, in the defense of your mother, you could play the role of the defense attorney who calls your mother to testify as a twelve-year-old girl about her childhood. Your questions and her answers could yield valuable information about how she grew up. Step two is a monologue from each parent as you imagine them defending themselves. Step three helps you put all this into a new context, using your own high witness to summarize the important lessons and learnings of the first two steps.

Witness for the Defense of Your Mother

In this part of the process, it is necessary for you to be able to see your mother as a twelve-year-old girl, as a witness who can describe her childhood. This is best done in a group setting where others can assist you by playing various witnesses or supporting your efforts. It is often helpful if you can play the part of your mother and have someone else take your role as a defense attorney. This aids in the development of empathy for your mother. The following is an example of a dialogue between a client, Jonathon, and his mother, Agnes. In this dialogue, Jonathon took the part of his mother (as a thirteen-year-old) and I took the defense attorney role.

Jonathon: Hello, Agnes. Tell us how it was between you and your parents.

Agnes: My parents were always fighting. I can't remember a time when they weren't fighting. I was always scared I would do or say something that would set one of them off. My father would get angry and send us all away. Mom and us kids would go and live with my aunt and uncle for months at a time. They lived about two miles down the road. Then Mom would talk to Dad and we never knew what they said, but usually after that we all could go home again until another fight would start.

Jonathon: That must have been awful. Did you ever know why the fights occurred?

Agnes: My father was always drinking and running around with other women. It started after he lost his arm in an accident on the farm. I was real small when that happened. I remember that he apparently got it caught in a thrashing machine somehow and they had to cut it off above the elbow. It was horrible. Everyone cried and cried and I was so scared because I didn't understand. After that, Dad would just sit in his chair and stare off in space for hours at a time. Mom told us not to disturb him so we stayed away from him. I often wanted to crawl up in his lap but I was too scared to approach him. He looked so lonely but also so angry that I didn't know what to do.

Jonathon: Did he ever do anything with you or for you?

Agnes: Yes, sometimes he would bring home candy for us kids and he seemed pleased that we were happy. But mostly he didn't come home. I could tell how worried Mom would get, but she never talked about any of this with me. She would not share her feelings with me. We were very poor and Mom had to go to work so we would have food to eat. We were all supposed to take care of ourselves somehow and not make any demands. I often cried myself to sleep worrying about what would happen to me and my family. I had to do many chores around the house after school and cook for my sisters and brothers when Mom was away.

Jonathon: It sounds like you never had a childhood and that you had to grow up long before you were ready to. How did you feel about that?

Agnes: I felt sad and resentful, like a victim of some crazy circumstances. I wondered why I was born sometimes. It all seemed so unfair. I hated it. These people who were my parents just couldn't take care of me. There was very little joy in my family. I never got to play and have fun like other kids my age.

Jonathon: I can see why you were always so scared and angry around me. I thought you hated me. Now I see you hated your parents and your situation and never got free from that hate.

Agnes: I tried to do what I could to help out, but most of the time no one even noticed or even said, "Thanks." There didn't seem to be any

149

option except to wait until you got old enough to be able to get married or leave somehow.

In this dialogue, Jonathon began to see his mother in a new light. Previously, in his prosecution of his mother, he expressed lots of anger at her for being so controlling and for making him feel afraid of the world and people. Now, in this defense dialogue, he began to see her differently and developed more understanding about why she behaved so negatively toward him. Other witnesses who were called (played by group members) were Agnes's father and mother and her older brother, who all added their perceptions of what went on during Agnes's childhood.

Mother's Own Defense

Step two involves your mother's own defense as an adult. Using our dialogue with Jonathon and Agnes as an example, we see that this step helped Jonathon see even more clearly who his mother really was and is today. Jonathon decided to speak again in the role of his mother, hoping to get even more insights. Jonathon speaking as Agnes says,

> From the way I grew up, I developed very low self-esteem. I didn't like myself very much because all I ever heard were messages of how bad I was and I believed it. I just kept quiet and suffered from loneliness, sadness and fear. I was even sexually molested by my grandfather, and he told me he would have me sent away to an orphanage if I ever told anyone. I never told anyone and I just tried to stay away from him.
>
> I had to quit school in eighth grade and go to work to earn money for the family. My father was unemployed most of the time and my mom worked hard for low wages. She wanted to be able to send my brother to college and so I had to help out more. I wanted to stay in school but I didn't say so. I was afraid they would send me to live with my aunt and uncle or my grandfather and grandmother.
>
> When I married Sam, I was happy to get away from my family, but that didn't turn out well either. Sam was sick a lot and he lost his job. I had to go to work again and then he also would sit and brood like my father did. He would shut me out like Dad did, too. In the middle of all this, I got pregnant with you, Jonathon, and worked as long as I could so we could have some

money when the baby came. When you were born, Jonathon, I had a hard time taking care of you. I got no support from anyone. My family had so many problems they couldn't help me much. Sam's family was quick to criticize me for everything and was always taking Sam's side. He could always run to his mother and get support, but I couldn't get any support. Sam seemed to be afraid of you, Jonathon, and he didn't want to be involved much, so it all fell on my shoulders. I couldn't stand the pressure and I stopped producing milk to nurse you, but I didn't want anyone to know. I kept trying and, after six weeks, you were losing weight and were not doing well.

I felt like a complete failure and I decided that Sam's mother should take over your care. We had no money so I thought if I went to work maybe it would take some of the worry and pressure off for me. I didn't see any other way to do this. I came to get you every weekend, but I sure wish I could have managed all that without letting Sam's mother raise you. I ended up feeling even worse about myself. When you were ten months old, Sam and I moved into a house his mother owned, and she allowed us to live there rent-free until we could get our feet on the ground financially.

I still had to work and I was scared of the responsibility of being your mother on a full-time basis, so we hired a local girl to take care of you while I worked. She was good to you and I felt better than when Sam's mother was taking care of you. I worked part-time later on and tried to spend more time with you. Sam was still unable to be with you much. He must have felt inadequate, too. Sam's father would come to visit and take you for walks. Sam's sister would buy you gifts, but I was jealous. I wanted to be able to buy you gifts, but I didn't have any money. It hurt me to see Sam's relatives making a fuss over you, and I felt like they were still trying to show me up and undermine my effectiveness as a mother. I used to get angry at you when you would come home with a new toy after visiting Sam's parents or his sister. I know you didn't know why I was so angry at you. I actually didn't know either at the time.

This monologue done by Jonathon brought him lots of insights about his mother and what was going on with her about the time he was born. He often felt confused about this period of his life.

He also had found it difficult in his adult life to settle down with one woman, often preferring to have close relationships with three women, although usually not sexual relationships. He came to understand that he had actually had three mothers before the age of one and apparently was unable to get what he needed from one mother alone. This monologue helped Jonathon to see how and why he got so confused in his relationships with women. Mostly it helped him see his mother, too, as a victim, and he had empathy for her feelings of helplessness and her low self-esteem.

In the final step of this defense of his mother, Jonathon had to summarize her defense in his own words from the standpoint of a high witness. A high witness is someone who is wise and just and sees the truth and meanings of these events. Jonathon's summarization began this way:

> I can now see that my mother was unable to handle the situation she was in and made some very courageous decisions. I can see how hard it would be for a mother to give up her own child because she saw that maybe he could get better care from someone else. This takes a special kind of unselfish love and devotion. She demonstrated a strength that many mothers would not have had. Also, when I realize that she was criticized for everything she did, I see what a tremendous risk she took. I'm sure that asking my grandmother to mother me saved my life. I probably would have become a failure-to-thrive baby and simply died. I was so angry and resentful at my mother for abandoning me that I never considered that her act may have saved my life.

With these new awarenesses, Jonathon can now begin to put more of the pieces together and reeducate himself. He has a more complete picture of what really happened to him and why it happened. He is ready to move to the next step in the process of reclaiming his true self and breaking the old karmic patterns that grew out of his incomplete picture of his childhood. Obviously, he must also go through the defense of his father, for much lies buried behind the walls of secrecy surrounding his father.

CHAPTER EIGHTEEN

Reintegration of New Thoughts and Feelings

There is as much difference between us and ourselves as between us and others.

—MICHAEL DeMONTAIGNE

If I Had Not Been Wounded

Most of the focus so far in this book has been on the negative effects of your narcissistic wounding during childhood. With this one-dimensional focus, you may miss many important awarenesses and learnings that are imbedded in your wounds. It is often in these weak places of unhealed wounds where your greatest opportunities for growth occur. Carl Jung said, rather cryptically, that it is the fourth door of your room where the angels enter. He meant that your weakest point, or area with the least awareness, is where your greatest lessons come from. He also said that the divine will enter your consciousness from what you despise.

As a way of reintegrating a fuller picture of what really happened to you during childhood, take another look at the major narcissistic wounds and ask yourself: "If I had not been wounded in this way, what would I have missed?" Or, ask it even more positively: "As a result of being wounded, what did I gain?" Make a list of the possible gains you made as a result of the wounds you received during childhood.

For example, I grew up in a family where there were many secrets. My need to know what was going on was not taken seriously.

As a result, I got good at figuring out how people were feeling and what kind of a mood they were in by observing closely their nonverbal behaviors. This skill is very useful for me now in my therapy work with people and in my own relationships. Also, I am a very sensitive person because of many woundings, but my sensitive nature also enables me to be sensitive to the feelings and woundings of other people. I can also empathize with the feelings of others quite easily because of my awareness of my own feelings growing out of my woundings.

Even major abandonments in childhood can have a positive side, showing you that you can survive major losses and abandonments. Every major disappointment, wounding or betrayal has built into it a positive gain in consciousness, an expansion of reality. The full recovery of your true self is aided by the development of a more balanced picture of your childhood. William James once said that if you have a real sense of your shadows and your light, then you will have full intelligence. Also, in order to move in consciousness, from operating under the laws of karma to operating under the laws of grace, requires that you balance all your parts. No parts of your consciousness can be dominant.

New Understanding of What Really Happened

Because you have just focused on your negative love experiences from childhood that were stuck in your body/mind, it is now necessary to focus on some of the positive emotional experiences of childhood. It is necessary to uncover and re-experience those moments from your childhood when your parents were affectionate, protective and caring with you. Even the most horrible childhood had moments of joy and positive human experiences.

Unlike the earlier prosecution of your parents, this requires no goading questions to get you started. In fact, when you have purged yourself of the old negativity, you should have no difficulty recalling positive scenes from your childhood. Sit with a pen and paper or a tape recorder and let your mind drift back to your childhood and start writing or talking.

I remember many good times I had at my grandmother's house, helping her bake pies and cakes. She always saved some of the leftover pie crust dough and allowed me to make a pie with it. To this day, the smell of pies baking brings back that memory. I also remember how my mother would cook a big meal on Sunday and on holidays, and the whole family would gather. Everyone seemed more relaxed and less rushed at Sunday dinner or on holidays. I can remember that as a small child I used to run my little trucks all over my uncle's back while he was taking a nap. Also, my aunt used to hold me and rub my head. She liked to run her hands through my blond curls, and it felt so relaxing and soothing to me. Even today, having my wife, Janae, rub my head is a special treat.

I have fond memories of working with my dad in his woodworking shop in the summertime. I helped him refinish furniture, and I enjoyed watching him make furniture and sensing the pride he took in his work. I remember feeling that same pride in the finish work I did on the furniture.

These are some examples of the kinds of positive memories you can begin to recall. In order to take the process even further now, begin to describe how your parents' virtues affected your life in positive ways. This helps you see positive traits in your parents that may have helped you grow and influenced you in positive ways. Again, if I use my own situation as an example, I can see that my father's love of antiques and history had a positive effect on me. I grew to love history from the many stories he would tell about the history of our local area, and I went on to study history and teach it for a while. I was also influenced by my father's love of opera, even though I made fun of him for it when I was a child. As I became older, I grew to appreciate fine music and opera, but as a child I was embarrassed for him because no one else I knew cared for opera. He also modeled independent thinking by this interest. He didn't go along with the crowd and was somewhat unconventional in a conventional sort of way. I see myself following this path as well in many things that I do.

My mother's drive to learn more and more influenced me. She went to beauty school when she was in her late thirties and was always trying to learn new techniques to use in her business. Even though she is now retired, she is always reading and open to new ideas. She is also a very generous person and gives of herself to others. She helped me learn the value of service.

If your parents are still alive, it is important to tell them the things you appreciate about them. If they live some distance from you, you can write them a letter or call them on the telephone, letting them know how much you appreciate them. Parents often are still carrying a lot of guilt about not being perfect parents and having caused you wounds, so this kind of message helps them to let go of their guilt and can certainly help you complete your letting-go process.

Feeling Compassion Toward Our Parents and Ourselves

Frequently, even though the anger and hostility are gone, there remains a deeper level of sadness that needs to be released as well. The prosecution, and particularly the defense, of your parents may bring up sadness toward your parents, but the full expression of sadness may need to be facilitated further. The following activity is designed to help bring up any further sadness and grief. In this process, it is necessary for you to imagine the death of each of your parents and to experience the emotions connected with their death. If we are able to see our parents as they really are, we usually feel sad about the unfulfilled lives of our parents. We see the tragedy of their limited lives. We see what they might have been or could have been compared to who they are.

The instructions in this activity are to imagine that each parent has just died, separately, and then write out or act out your deepest feelings about your parent's death. Experience what others might say about your mother or father, and experience their funeral and burial, letting the full force of your sad feelings come out. If your parents have already died, you may recall how you felt then or pretend it is happening now and relive your feelings in the present. Again, since both of my parents are still alive, I will use my own process as an example.

> I get home from my office and my wife tells me that she received a call that my father died today of a stroke. I feel a sinking feeling in my body and I have to sit down. Tears come as I think of him and my love for him. I think of all the fun times we had together playing tennis and joking around. I can see his smile and the twinkle in his eyes just before he tells a joke or says something funny. I will miss him and all the little things about him that I came to love and understand. He was a proud man but very humble. His generous, gentle nature was disarming to many. He was always friendly and, even though he was also shy, he would greet strangers and make people feel very welcomed in his house. I'm sad that he didn't get to travel more and meet

people from other cultures. I'm sad that he didn't get to go back to visit his European roots. He talked of doing that, but he waited too long.

He loved to make furniture. He was so talented with his hands and he got very little recognition for his work, but that didn't seem to matter. He just loved working with his hands and making fine furniture.

I'm glad for all the good times we had together, but I am so sad that I won't have any more good times with him. He is gone and with him goes my love for him. Life is so short. We only really got to know each other in the past eight or nine years. We missed so much we could have done together. Why did you have to die so soon?

The completion of this activity with both your parents can bring you in touch with deep feelings of sadness and incomplete processes. If your parents are still alive, you can complete what is still incomplete with them directly. I remember having this experience with my grandmother just before her death. My mother had called to tell me my grandmother was dying but she might last a week or two more. Since she lived two thousand miles away, I could not leave to be with her for another week, so I quickly wrote a letter to her and expressed all the things I wanted to say to her. Then I went to see her and she said everything she wanted to say to me.

Then she didn't die, but got much better for a while. It was a wonderful experience to spend time with her after that, knowing that everything was complete between us. Several months later, she died quietly in her sleep, and I felt a sense of sadness but no regrets. This experience reminded me of many relationships where I don't feel a sense of completion, and it led me to consciously work to bring about completion in more of my relationships.

CHAPTER NINETEEN

Finding Your True Self

Unless you are willing to forgive your parents, you will not grow up.
—BARRY WEINHOLD

Surrender, Acceptance and Forgiveness

Your family patterns survive mainly on the hope that some-day your parents will change their ways and begin to love you the way you have always wanted. No matter how much you struggle to get your parents to change, you will never get them to give you un-conditional love. Why? Because they don't have it to give and proba-bly never will. One empty cup cannot fill another one. The only way to recover what was lost is to find it inside yourself and stop the end-less search for love from your parents, or parent substitutes like spouses or children. Learning to love yourself is aided by completing these final steps of surrender, acceptance (apotheosis) and forgiveness.

Surrender

Surrender has two sides—a masculine and a feminine. Both are im-portant for surrender to be effective. The feminine side of surrender involves a willingness to receive without resistance. This means being willing to take in or receive what is real, and not only those things that you like. It involves seeing your parents or your spouse exactly as they are and not resisting any part of them because you don't like that part or wish they would change that part. This wish to have others change to suit your needs and preferences ignores the fundamental truth, which is that they are not going to change something about themselves unless *they* want to. It also means seeing yourself in this way as well. What you resist in others and in yourself is what usually persists in your life.

This openness, however, is only valuable when you are able to utilize the masculine side of surrender, which is the willingness to take control without guilt. This means you have to take charge of your life without feeling guilty that you are robbing your parents or someone else of the job. Many people feel guilty when they take charge of their life. They are afraid they will be rejected or be seen as rejecting if they no longer need the other person to be responsible. Old patterns can surely keep people tied to dependencies, fearing to become independent. The willingness to go on internal power, so to speak, then makes use of the feminine side of surrender to let go of old attachments and open up to receiving people as they really are. If you over–develop the feminine side, you remain open to receive everything but cannot use any of what you receive to help yourself get on with your life. Those who over-develop the masculine side of surrender are ready to take charge of their life but often are not open to receiving the vital information they need to help them go forward. In both of these situations, a person remains stuck, unable to move without purpose. These steps involve profound advances in consciousness that enable you to have struggle-free, loving relationships with people.

Acceptance

This follows surrender and really is the manifestation of the principles of surrender. Acceptance means giving up any and all claims to try to change or punish your parents and releasing them from blame, allowing them to find their highest good on their own. It also means learning to accept yourself, which may be much more difficult than accepting others. Self-acceptance also means entering into apotheosis, which involves a great taking up of the undeserved into the unqualified. In many ways, the journey to break your family patterns is a spiritual journey. It leads you toward a reunion with your true self.

Reuniting The Divided Self: Apotheosis

This activity should be completed with a partner who will read the instructions and can lead you in the activity. It is helpful to prepare yourself for this step by putting on some favorite soft music for the background as well as burning incense or lighting a candle to help ritualize the process. You may feel like you are in an altered state of consciousness during this activity, so relax yourself, staying open to whatever happens.

Have your partner read the following instructions slowly while you close your eyes and relax:

I am about to ask you to review your life. Begin by thinking about your day. Go back to when you woke up this morning. Try to remember a sequence of events that happened today. Use as many of your senses as you can: see the events, hear what was said, taste and smell and feel what happened . . . Now go back to something that happened to you last week and recall as vividly as possible what happened . . . Now go back to the past month . . . Now to the past year . . . Recall an event as vividly as possible . . . Now go back five years and recall some important or unimportant event . . . Go back even further now, to your college years, or the time just after high school, and remember an event from your life at that time . . . Now go back to high school . . . to junior high school . . . to elementary school . . . to when you entered school . . . Recall your first day in school . . . How did you feel? What happened to you? . . . Now go back further to when you were a pre-school child and remember an event from your life . . . now back to when you were two years old . . . a baby . . . Now go back to the time of your birth and remember, allowing whatever memory traces you have to emerge . . . Now go back to the time you were still in your mother's womb . . . and finally go back to a time before your conception . . . In your unborn state, imagine you are about to meet your double, your own true self that you gave up or lost somewhere before you grew up . . . Experience your double standing in front of you, facing you . . . Dialogue with your true self. Get acquainted again. Breathe with your true self and build a rhythm between the two of you . . . When you feel connected again with your true self, feel yourself merging with him or her so you feel and see the two of you together . . . When you feel this union, begin to re-experience each of the events of your life, this time reunited with your true self, putting aside the old masks and false selves you used to hide your true self . . . Start with re-experiencing your time in the womb, this time remembering being united and whole . . . Now

160

re-experience your birth . . . Watch now for the pressures to put away your true self and guard against this . . . Now re-experience your life up to age two, this time keeping your union with your true self . . . Now up to age five or six . . . Now your first day in school . . . Now up to age twelve . . . Now through junior high school . . . and on through high school . . . Now to college or up to about age twenty-two . . . Now up to five years ago . . . Now one year ago . . . Now last month . . . last week . . . and finally, come back to present time, still being reunited with your true self. When you are ready, slowly open your eyes and bring your attention to focus on your surroundings.

This activity has produced profound insights and integrative experiences for people with whom I have used it. Some people remember the exact moment when they gave up their true self. Often, when they come back to this moment, they find they can withstand the pressures and maintain their union. Others come back with a renewed sense of who they really are and are able to integrate that knowledge with their false self or who they thought they had to be.

Forgiveness

Forgiveness has gotten some bad press as a useful concept, and rightfully so. The religious use of the term has failed to stem the tide of hatred and war in the world. The use of forgiveness usually denies the truth of our feelings and only deflects the anger but does not do away with it.

True forgiveness does not deny or deflect anger but faces it head on. In the prosecution of your parents, you could feel outraged at the injustices you suffered at their hands and recognize that what happened to you was not for your own good, but to allow them to get revenge. Only if you can feel hatred toward your parents for all this, is the path to true forgiveness open to you. When your hatred and anger are expressed completely, they usually get transformed into feelings of sorrow and pain at being treated so poorly. If this sorrow and pain is expressed as well, it leads you to a genuine understanding of your parents and why they treated you this way. This understanding leads you to feel genuine empathy and sympathy toward your parents as victims themselves, which makes forgiveness a natural act of grace that is not produced by some religious rules or commandments.

161

You can deal with forgiveness either directly with your parents or symbolically, if they are dead or otherwise unavailable for direct communication. The forgiveness in either case is for your benefit and not theirs. If you do this process symbolically, it is good to picture each parent sitting in front of you as you do this. You can also dialogue with them using an empty chair or pillows, or act out a dialogue using friends. The process of forgiveness has five important steps (Weinhold & Andersen 1979):

1. Forgiving your parents (directly or symbolically).
2. Forgiving yourself.
3. Giving up all claims to punish your parents or yourself.
4. Releasing your parents and yourself from your previous relationship.
5. Restoring a harmonious relationship with your parents and yourself.

These five steps enable you to do some final clearing work on any old patterns that may still exist in your unconscious.

Forgiving Your Parents

A good way to test yourself is to go back through your written prosecution of your parents and pick out the key "crimes" for which you felt they should be punished. (Ex: "Mother, you never told me that you loved me.") Then take each of these crimes and write a statement of forgiveness. (Ex: "I now forgive you, Mother, for not telling me that you loved me. I now realize that you didn't know how to love.") Notice any resistance that surfaces during this activity. That is an indication that you are still holding on to some resentment. It is good to use a response column on your paper to the right of your written forgiveness statements. Here you can record any resistant thoughts and feelings.

Complete those that you can complete without resistance, and then go back and work with your resistance. You may go back to prosecuting them some more and then building a new defense before working more on forgiveness. It is important not to force it; that will drive any remaining resentment further away from your consciousness. Take your time and complete this step over a period of time or in stages.

Forgiving Yourself

This is important so you can make sure you haven't taken on the sins of your parents and are now using them to still beat yourself up. If you find you are more critical of yourself than of others, it is likely you have taken on some of your parents' issues. Forgiveness in this context means to "give back" to your parents or others that which belongs to them and not to you. Again, write out each self-forgiveness statement and use a response column to process any resistance. (Ex: "I now forgive myself for believing that I was unlovable.")

Giving Up Wishes to Punish

A desire to punish your parents or yourself indicates that you are still carrying resentment about something. This step gives you another opportunity to explore your depths for any remaining resentment to be cleared. Recall the areas where you previously had resentments and use them as part of a written statement. (Ex: "I now give up all claims to punishing you, Mother, for not telling me that you loved me when I was a child. I now acknowledge my love for you and yours for me.") Notice again if any resistance to doing this occurs. (Ex: "This is stupid; I don't need to do this any more.") Also, be sure to check out any resentments you may be holding against yourself. (Ex: "I give up all claims to punishing myself for feeling unlovable.")

Releasing Your Parents and Yourself

This is a final goodbye to the old relationship that you and your parents maintained. Many times, we may have cleared our patterns but still maintain a subconscious illusion about the old relationships we had with each other. The real test, of course, is being able to be in the presence of your parents for a length of time and not regress back to the old relationship patterns. In my work with people, I often send them on fact-finding visits with their parents to help them determine how the patterns operate and to experience how they can get pulled into the old ways of relating. As they get clear of their patterns, they can spend more time with their parents without getting hooked back into the old relationships. This step acknowledges that the old relationship is over for you. (Ex: "I now release you, Mother, from the relationship we had in the past and encourage you to develop your self in any way you choose.")

Restoring Harmony

This step is designed to help you further support your new relationship with your parents and with yourself. First, write down all the things you appreciate about yourself and are grateful for in yourself. After you have done that and cleared any resistance, do the same for each of your parents. You may want to send a letter containing these statements of appreciation and gratitude to yourself and to each of your parents.

All of these steps are part of a healing process for you and maybe for your parents and your children as well. Once you have completed this process, you will have restored harmony to your life, but that does not mean that disharmony can't come back. The difference is, if it does, you now have many tools to work with and can clear away any barriers rather quickly and move on. The next chapter will present a number of specific tools you can use to work on your self and continue this process for the rest of your life, full of confidence that no matter what happens to you in your lifetime, *you now have resources to work with to continue your growth and evolution as a conscious being.* There is tremendous satisfaction and joy in reaching this level of relationship with yourself and with others.

CHAPTER TWENTY

Tools for Strengthening Your True Self

... the human soul is virtually indestructible and its ability to rise from the ashes remains as long as the body draws breath.

—ALICE MILLER

This chapter consists of a number of tools and techniques for strengthening your connection with your true self. Most of these are designed to be used in groups, but some can be adapted for use with pairs or couples and when working alone.

The Love Seat

(Hills 1980) This is a structured group activity that can be used with people who either know each other or are meeting for the first time. The goal of the love seat is to overcome hostility and suspicion and to build trust among members of a group by encouraging openness and trust in communication. The process shows people that honesty and an atmosphere of mutual respect can lead to deeper relationships. This activity is also very useful for groups of people who work together.

The process goes like this. One person is chosen to sit in the center of the circle (the love seat). This individual faces each person in the perimeter of the circle, and each of them on the perimeter tells the person in the love seat one thing he or she likes most about that individual, and one thing he or she thinks needs to be changed in order for that person to grow. The person in the love seat cannot reply until everyone on the perimeter has spoken. Next, the love-seater says one thing he/she likes best about him/herself and one thing he/she feels he/she has to work on. Someone takes notes, recording all that is said. Then the love-seater may comment on the feedback. The position of the love seat usually is rotated until everyone has sat in the love seat, or, by prior agreement, the process can be limited to one person at each group meeting.

The next step is to look at the feedback to see if it was a projection or a direct perception. Usually a group consensus is decided. A projection is when the feedback was more true for the person who gave it than the one receiving it, although it can be about fifty-fifty, which is a "semi-projection." If the feedback applies mostly to the receiver of it and not the sender, it is seen more as a direct perception. The feedback is read by the recorder and discussed. This helps everyone become more aware of the differences between projections and direct perceptions. Questions such as "How accurate was the feedback overall?" or "How can we make the process more productive?" help the group sharpen the process. Being mirrored in this way by a group committed to telling the truth can help strengthen your own perceptions about who you are.

Deep Empathy

This is another mirroring exercise that can be done in pairs or in a group. A pair sits facing each other. (In a group, pairs take turns doing this while the others observe what is happening.) One person of the pair tells how he/she feels about him/herself right now and how he/she feels about the relationship with the other person in the pair (and the group, if done in a group setting). The other person in the pair listens with an open mind to the impressions, feelings and thoughts of the other. The listener concentrates on taking in all that is said until he/she can empathize with the other person so strongly that the feelings, impressions and thoughts seem like one's own rather than belonging to the other.

Then the listener starts to mirror back to the first person the way he/she feels this person to be as he/she is experiencing him/her right now. If the listener does not feel identified enough, he/she can ask questions until he/she feels identified. It is good to videotape this process so afterward the listener can see what was love or empathy and what was projection. Also the basic assumptions the listener makes about the talker are made visible. This activity can help you learn how to experience in depth the inner world of another person, seeing beneath the mask of the personality and the patterns. Seeing the essence of another person and mirroring that for them can be a true act of friendship and love.

Writing About Objects

(Weinhold 1984) This is a simple but powerful exercise that can be done alone. Find an object that is dark, earthy and organic and that catches your attention. It could be a dead leaf or a moss-covered rock or a piece of tree bark or just a clump of dirt. Describe the object, using all of your senses that you can. What is its shape? How large is it? What does it smell like? What color is it? Where have I seen that color before? What is the texture of the object? Feel it, smell it, even taste it if you can, and then describe it even further. Use cross-sensing to describe it. What color does it sound like? What does its texture smell like? What does its smell feel like?

Next, use the object to uncover any psychological meaning. Compare the object with some aspects of your mother or your father. What of your father or your mother do you see represented in this object? Then, *become* the object. Ask, "What can this object tell or show me about myself that I need to know?" What about the object reminds you of your childhood?

On an imaginary level, create a myth or story about the object. You can make up a new myth or relate it to an existing myth. What about the object reminds you of a mythic figure?

Finally, you can use the object to help you understand your "Ground of Being" or God elements. You can describe the object as God (using your own interpretation) and elaborate on the God-like elements of the object. Below is a description of an object that I worked with in this way. It was a fallen seed pod from a locust tree.

> I am a proud and lofty being, but I must overcome that pride and surrender to forces much wiser than I. I realize that I must give up trying to control my relationships. It is foolish to think I can do that, anyway. I can't grow any more from this proud and lofty position, so I have fallen to the earth. Here I can become a humble figure in a long, dark brown robe. I can now serve others and give up all the ego needs I have used to gratify and satisfy myself. I know how to do that.

I looked again at this seed pod and saw a figure that must be able to become a fool. This figure must be able to be a fool in order to grow and has to become an object of ridicule by the people of the earth. I heard others saying, "Look at that silly man in the brown robe. He is dumb; look at him trying to serve others—isn't that stupid. Who does he think he is? He is just a mystic, a crackpot. He can't possibly amount to anything. Look at him there on the ground; he is weak and helpless and people can step on him. You'd think he would know better. What a jerk! I don't want to be around that much stupidity. He is dangerous, look at him—we'll have to kill him. He can't act that way. Who does he think he is?" I reflected on this question and the words that came to me were, "I am love and I am real and I am God! Thank you for asking me who I am."

Process-Oriented Psychology

(Mindell 1985) A new approach to psychology, developed by Dr. Arnold Mindell of Zurich, Switzerland, called Process-Oriented Psychology, can be used to promote more integration. The theory, which is a combination of information theory, field theory and systems theory, works by identifying the various channels (visual, auditory, kinesthetic, proprioceptive, relationship and world) by which we take in information. These form into primary processes and secondary processes. The primary process is usually conscious and identifiable, but the secondary processes are often unconscious and not readily available.

Identifying a main channel, and amplifying whatever is going on there until the channel switches to another one, is usually the way to activate the secondary process. This often helps to bring unconscious material to the surface so it can be better integrated into consciousness. This process can be used to bring more and more elements of your true self into awareness. Your secondary process is where your true self resides, and your primary process carries your adapted patterns and your false self. Frequently, the secondary process shows up in dreams and body symptoms, or is split off and projected onto another person in a relationship. In Process-Oriented Psychology this secondary process is often called the Dreambody.

Usually people have borders beyond which they are afraid to go in exploring their secondary processes. By learning to identify your boundary lines, you can begin to see where your primary process can be expanded to where your secondary process takes over. Most of the time, people are afraid of their secondary processes, and they get to the edge of their awareness and back away. They say, "I can't do this." So try the following experiment by asking yourself these questions and write down your answers:

1. What can you almost not bear to look at in your life?
2. What can you almost not bear to hear?
3. What feelings seem too much for you to feel?
4. What movements seem to be forbidden to you?
5. What relationship problems or issues would you like to avoid?
6. What kind of people are hard for you to be around?
7. What world problems bother you the most?

After you identify a limiting edge in yourself, you can begin to know where you need to work on yourself. All of our family patterns existed outside our awareness at one time, so they exist in our secondary process. The edges you identified are gateways into your unconscious family patterns. In order to go over the edge into the unknown territory, all you need to do is amplify the channel where the edge is until the channel changes. The new channel will usually yield new information for you to work with, and you can learn to integrate it into your main channels or primary process.

Arny Mindell tells the story of a client who had a chronic bladder and prostate problem. This man decided to work along on his symptoms through meditation. He was in meditation when he felt his bladder hurting. He tried amplifying the problem by continuing to meditate and not urinating, even though the doctors had warned him not to do that. As he sat and sat, his bladder felt like it was going to burst, and he feared he might die if it did. (This was an edge for him.) He continued to amplify his fear of dying until he saw himself (channel change) filled with a red substance like a balloon getting ready to burst from holding in all his inhibitions. As a result of this insight, he reported feeling an immense freedom and happiness. After taking several deep breaths, he got up and began to dance and cry tears of happiness, for he knew he had conquered his fear of dying. He saw that his bladder problems were his Dreambody trying to get him to loosen up and live. When he went over his edge by amplifying his fear of death, he found out why the symptom was there. Once he knew its purpose, he no longer needed the symptom any more. (Mindell 1985)

Frequently, body symptoms and diseases are ways the body is trying to help us do something that we need to do but haven't been aware of.

PSYCHODRAMA

This is a powerful therapeutic technique developed in the 1920s by J. L. Moreno. It was originally used to enable people to release their feelings and help uncover internal blocks. In the chapter called *The Prosecution of Your Parents,* I suggested several psychodramatic approaches. This technique can also be utilized as an integrative tool to help you strengthen your connection with your true self. In this way, psychodrama can enable a group of people who are working on integration to get clearer pictures of themselves. As present or past scenes from your life are acted out, using others to play internal parts of you (your true self or your adapted self, etc.) or play other people in your life, you have a chance to sort out your own projections from true perceptions. Everyone learns from this process.

Frequently in psychodrama you can go deeper into issues than in your real life and find the deeper meanings. Special techniques include use of an alter ego or a double where one or more people stand with or behind a person to reinforce what he or she is trying to express. Often the alter ego can speak for the person who may be temporarily stuck or in need of a new perspective. The double can actually replace the person working so he or she can see him/herself as the double sees him/her. Also, group members can play an ideal other, or how the person working would like himself to be, or how he would like his spouse, parent, friend, co-workers, etc. to be. This again gives the person who is working a chance to see his/her ideal in action in order to decide how to integrate that projected part.

Gestalt Techniques

Like psychodrama, Gestalt therapy techniques can be useful for the integrative work of strengthening your connections with your true self. One of the most common techniques involves the use of an empty chair or a pillow where you can dialogue with a part of yourself, a dream figure or another person in your life. It is often useful in sharpening distinctions between your true self and your adapted self, or in seeing some unintegrated part of you more clearly. This works by putting the split-off part on an empty chair or a pillow and telling that part how you think or feel about them. You then switch chairs and

170

reply as you think the split-off part might reply, thus building more understanding of that part's perspective. The dialogue continues, with you playing both parts, until a better understanding or some integration is reached.

The Missionary's Child

The following example is presented to illustrate how a combination of process-oriented psychology and psychodrama was used to help a client break an old family pattern. The client, Jean, tells her story.

My parents belonged to a strict fundamentalist Christian church, and in our small town everyone was expected to follow the church dogma. As a little girl, I watched my parents enjoy the envy of their friends for their missionary activities. They used almost all the family's energy, money, talents and skills to help underprivileged children in other lands. We were all denied everything, including love.

When I was six years old, I started earning money selling fruits and vegetables to our neighbors out of my little red wagon. I also helped to clean houses and babysat to earn money for camp. When my father discovered my little stash of savings, he told me he would put it in the bank at his office for safe keeping. So every week I would hand him my money to put in the bank at the office. About age ten or eleven, I asked him one day if I could have some of my money to buy a bicycle. I had kept track and knew I had $214 saved up. He said he would check with the bank and let me know the next day. When he came home from the office the next day, I asked him for my money. He said smilingly, "Well, dear Jean, you gave all your money to the missionaries yesterday." I stood there dumbfounded, disbelieving that my father had betrayed me this way. I just burst into tears and turned away.

I had actually forgotten that incident until recently, and now I see this pattern of turning my money and my power over to men. I have been married four times. In each case, I was betrayed by my husband over my money. I wrote a best-selling book and my husband took all the royalties, and many other similar incidents happened where I thought I was an innocent victim of these cruel men.

I joined a therapy group after my fourth marriage collapsed, and one night I decided to work on my feelings. I started my work by re-enacting a scene from my last marriage where again

171

my husband took all my savings to pay an income tax debt. While re-enacting this scene, I was asked if this had happened to me before, and suddenly I remembered what happened with my father when I was ten. I realized that I never got my feelings out and they were causing me to unconsciously set up similar situations.

Barry decided that I needed to prosecute my father for his betrayal and all the other things he did that I took like a 'good little girl.' Barry played my father and we re-enacted the scene from my childhood. He did such a good job that I soon felt this anger welling up in me. With the support of the group, I turned on Barry and tackled him, pinning him down, and started strangling him while screaming obscenities at him, telling him that I hated him and wished he were dead. Barry shifted as he saw I really meant business and apologized for his deed of long ago. I stopped strangling him because that is what I wanted to hear.

I made a decision in that group to never again give away my power or my money to a man. I realize now how much pain I have caused myself by not dealing with my feelings toward my father. This work was a big risk for a good little girl like me, but well worth it. Apparently, the only relationship pattern I have had with men is the one I learned from my father, and it kept me in my 'little girl' role all my life. I am now dating again and I notice how very aware I am of the pattern, and I am now finally learning new relationship patterns for being with men.

CHAPTER TWENTY-ONE

Breaking My Family Patterns

Elements of My Transformational Journey

I am going to share with you my journey to break my own family patterns. Where possible, I will refer to the transformational journey described in Chapter 7 and to patterns I have consciously broken. I became conscious of many patterns through my own therapy, books I have read and workshops I have attended.

I was the first-born son of upwardly mobile, Pennsylvania German, working-class parents. It was 1937, the middle of the great Depression. My father was an auto mechanic and my mother was a machine operator in a hosiery mill in a small town in southeastern Pennsylvania. Neither had graduated from high school, but both wanted me to get an education so I could escape the manual labor trap. My father was twenty-three and my mother twenty-one when I was born, and they probably were not prepared to handle the responsibility of parenting. Since my mother worked at this time, I was cared for by my paternal grandmother from the time I was six weeks old until I was ten months old. At that time, my parents hired a Mennonite girl to care for me full-time. I was a playpen baby and got no support for being independent. I was rewarded for being an obedient, good boy. Because I was the first-born, male grandchild, I was the one

173

under primogeniture rules who was to inherit the family fortune. Since there was no fortune, what I inherited instead was my family's fears about the world. They believed the world was a scary and unsafe place and certainly made sure I learned this "truth." As a result, I took very few risks to explore this scary world and remained under their protective care. I developed a "false self" to please them.

I was the first child, so my growth wasn't compared to any other sibling. However, their appetite for my performances seemed unending. I recall that when I was three years old, the whole extended family gathered to make a recording of me reciting nursery rhymes and telling stories about what I had seen at the Fall Farm Show. I was traumatized by this event, which led me to decide that I could never do enough to please them. I built a bubble or shield around myself and became a spectator of life, a pattern that I did not become conscious of until I was in my middle twenties.

I spent my first five years being treated as the special child in the extended family, only to have that world shattered by the birth of my sister. I remember not wanting to go home from my grandmother's house when my mother and baby sister came home from the hospital.

School opened up a new vista, but my lack of risk–taking caused me to hold back there as well. In junior high school, I started to come out of my shell and I fell in love with my childhood playmate. Again my world was shattered when she moved at the end of the eighth grade to a town 2,500 miles away. I never saw her again. I went back into my shell and again hid from the world. My next diversion was assuming the parenting role for my two-year-old brother. I was the built-in baby-sitter and gradually assumed more and more of a parenting role. I don't remember much about my relationship with my brother during this time, but today we are not close.

In ninth grade I took another risk and tried out for the basketball team. I was cut because I was too short. My main goal during the next year was to grow and I did. I grew eight inches in one year and this time was chosen for the team. This was my admission ticket back to belonging, being one of the jocks at school. I remember how important this was to me. I felt almost real again. This was the first goal I ever actually set and reached myself without help from anyone else. This was preparation for answering the call later.

Another milestone in high school was deciding to join a fraternal organization where I didn't know anyone. I surprised myself. I made friends with lots of young men and, within two years I became the leader of the organization and won their highest award for service. I was starting to believe in myself again, although I had recurring thoughts of death at the same time. I had convinced myself that I would not live to be twenty-one.

My college choice was a curious set of pluses and minuses. My parents had me tested when I was three or four to see if I was college material. The psychologist said that I was, so my parents often bragged to friends about setting aside money to send me to college. When the time came for me to go, I found out there was no money. They had spent it on my mother's beautician training. I was hurt and angry. After all the talk, there was no follow-through. All I could afford was to go to the local teachers' college. I worked that summer on a paint construction crew and earned enough money to afford to live in the dorm.

Near the end of my sophomore year, I met Fran, who was a senior in high school and from a higher social class than I was used to. Her parents made me feel special and I learned a lot about social graces that I never learned at home. After three years of dating, Fran and I were married—a marriage of convenience. I wanted to get away from home and she wanted to fulfill a dream of her parents that she would marry a college man.

After teaching high school social studies for three years, I got a chance to become a junior high school guidance counselor. I loved the challenge, but knew I needed more training. I talked to my old college advisor who recommended that I go to graduate school at the University of Minnesota. I applied and was accepted for a M.A. in Counseling. I took a leave of absence from my job, and Fran and I headed to the big city and a whole new life. Not bad for a kid who was afraid to risk. I got urbanized, traumatized, humanized and radicalized in my five years in Minnesota.

My Call to Awaken

My whole value system was turned upside-down because it was here that I decided to answer the call to live. I remember it as a very conscious choice. I had become painfully aware of the bubble I lived in, never being close to anyone. My bubble was almost burst one day when, in a group therapy class, my professor confronted me saying, "Barry, I don't think you are close to anyone." He saw through my

175

mask and I was terrified. Where could I hide? I was furious with him and yet I knew this was a call to awaken. Other events in my life all pointed the same way. I was miserable and I knew it. I had to do something drastic.

My Decision to Enter Life

I had to decide to stop being just a spectator and begin to live and take risks like everyone else. The decision was irreversible. I could not get enough of life and my experimentation with life had moved into high gear. I took steps to make changes in my marriage, started therapy, had an affair and, as a result, began to feel more and more alive. This was also a time of much social and political unrest, with the assassination of John Kennedy, the Vietnam war, protests, lies and much confusion. I began to be influenced by the protest music and theatre.

In the spring of 1968, while I was interviewing for a job in Detroit, Martin Luther King was shot, and while I was in Ohio for another job interview, Robert Kennedy was killed. My first position after completing my Ph.D. was at Ohio University in 1968. This was a university of 22,000 students in the middle of a town of 12,000 in the middle of nowhere. Rumblings from nearby Kent State were already being felt, and by that spring, I was involved in supporting a group of black students who wanted a black studies program. Also, we had student uprisings that brought National Guard troops with fixed bayonets to our campus. My marriage barely survived another crisis and now with two small children, Margie and Mark, we searched for a way to restore a healthy relationship. Again therapy and struggle were the best choices.

However, the biggest challenge to my young career came when I supported a young doctoral student who was denied an assistantship because he wore a beard. Actually, the issue went deeper than that and involved fear of group counseling. This doctoral student had taught a group dynamics course to teacher trainees using experiential methods, and this was threatening to the dean and others who feared personal encounters. By defending this student, I put my own job on the line and I knew I probably would have been fired if I had not found another job. As a parting shot, I printed a letter to all faculty members exposing what I saw as unethical actions of the dean and some colleagues. Again I realized I had faced another crisis and ended

176

up landing on my feet. All this was preparation for what was to come.

I was appointed Director of Counseling at the new University of Wisconsin campus at Green Bay. We opened our doors with about five thousand students on five different campus locations, and I plunged into the most intense period of creativity I had ever experienced. I remember the chancellor telling me when I was hired, "You are in charge of the mental health of this university." Only God Him/ Herself could have handled that job, but it was again a time of intense preparation. It wasn't long before my innovative program and practices got me embroiled in controversy.

My Death in Life Experience

Before I tell that part of the story, I want to interject a story of personal transformation that occurred while I was at Green Bay. It was to have far-reaching effects in my life. This is the story of my experience of my own death. The complete story is told in Chapter 12 of this book, so you may want to reread it before going on with this. The effects of that experience have continued to shape my life. I mark it as the beginning of my transpersonal search. I realized that nothing I had learned about psychology could help me understand this experience. It started in me a process of searching for answers to life and death questions and led me to question all that I had learned about human behavior. It was a vital step in my decision to answer the call to awaken. I remember that I had very few people I could talk to about this experience, so my search became solitary and isolated for some time to come.

At Green Bay, the vice-chancellor of the university, who had hired me, got fired and now I had to report directly to the chancellor. He seemed uncomfortable with the innovative approach I had developed, but he was unable to talk directly about his feelings. He would invite me to his office to chat about things in general, but these were often cordial, intellectual discussions. One day I received a five-page memo from him ordering me to cease all my innovative programs. I wrote a strong memo back and asked to talk to him about this, but he refused. I told him if we couldn't resolve this conflict, he should consider getting himself another Director of Counseling. Much was happening on campus to keep him occupied, so I thought the crisis might have passed, until one Sunday evening in December my Assistant Director asked to talk to me at the office. I went over to the university and he told me that the chancellor had fired me as Director and he was to be named as my successor at the end of the school year. I was devastated, hurt and scared, but with the help of friends and family I pulled myself together and began job hunting. For some time, nothing suitable was available, but finally a counselor education position at the University of Colorado–Colorado Springs opened up. I interviewed and accepted the position, starting a new phase of my journey.

As I looked back on my Green Bay experience, I saw that my inability to find effective ways to deal with authority was behind what happened. I never imagined getting fired and naively assumed that the conflict would go away and nothing would come of it. My own passivity and inaction set up the situation. My family pattern was to act weak and helpless and expect parental figures to take care of me. It was one of the ways I survived in my family of origin, but now this pattern was causing me a lot of trouble. Unfortunately, this pattern was imbedded in my unwillingness to accept full responsibility for my life and was destined to continue to draw problems to me.

Shortly after coming to Colorado, I got involved in a training program in transactional analysis and, as part of the program, I had to have a number of hours of therapy. While I was involved in the training, I began to see some of the holes in my development stemming back to childhood, so I decided to work on these issues in a group therapy setting where people were being re-parented. This led me to do intensive work on my family of origin issues for a period of about four years. I found that I had bonding problems and lots of resistance to bonding with my contract mother. (A contract mother is a therapist with whom a client commits to work through re–parenting issues.) I also found out that I was co-dependent and stuck in the separation process as well and had to learn healthy ways to separate once the bonding was resolved. Because I was an only child for my first five years, I also had to learn how to interact with siblings. I completed my therapy with many of my major issues from childhood either re-solved or with tools to continue work on them.

I was still somewhat co-dependent in my primary relationship. We had explored most aspects of the relationship and still felt that there were more patterns we hadn't uncovered.

I seemed to be searching for allies to help me sort it out. I read many books, attended workshops, went through therapy and finally, it was an encounter with a student in one of my classes that provided me with the key learning. One evening after class, there was the usual group of students huddled around me asking questions about the lecture or an assignment. After all the questions were answered and they had departed, I noticed one student was still there.

Her name was Barbara and she was returning to school after almost twenty years. She was a young-looking forty-year-old dressed in jeans and a shirt, with long blond hair. She spoke hesitantly as she tried to tell me something that was difficult to say. When I failed to understand her, she finally blurted out, "I want to be your friend." I was moved to tears by her words. I don't think anyone had ever said those words to me and it opened up an old, unhealed wound. My heart leaped with excitement and anticipation, so I arranged to meet Barbara for lunch the following week.

This was the beginning of a ten-year friendship that was the most complete human relationship I had ever experienced. Since we were both married at the time we met, we were just friends who enjoyed talking to each other, sometimes for hours, about our thoughts and ideas. Although neither of us wanted to admit it, we were falling in love with each other. Clearly, our relationship helped me open up my feminine side in ways I didn't know possible. I began to write poetry, learn to do creative art and literally come alive. Life took on a whole new meaning for me. Barbara seemed to use the relationship to develop her masculine side, as well as for asking me to help her clear up her own parenting issues with her children. The relationship took many twists and turns over the ten years, but first and foremost it was an important, transformational friendship.

One of the most important influences on my life began during a sabbatical leave from the University in 1977. I went to California and took a three-week intensive workshop on Lomi Bodywork, which was very integrative training in aikido, yoga, movement therapy, breath work, body work, meditation, diet and nutrition, and gestalt therapy. It was during that workshop that I became a vegetarian, and I mark that time as the preparation for crossing the threshold. While I was in California, I attended the Association for Humanistic Psychology conference at Berkeley where I heard two people give talks: Jean Houston and Leonard Orr. Both of these people had profound effects on me. They were very different speakers and yet both seemed to speak to something within me that was wanting to come out. I knew I wanted to study with each of them. I taped the Orr speech and listened to it over and over, each time finding more than the last time. He was talking about Rebirthing, a new growth tool involving breathing. Shortly after returning to Colorado, I had a client go into a spontaneous rebirth experience in one of my therapy groups, and I had the opportunity to midwife her rebirth even though I had no training in this process.

Within two months, I was on my way back to California to be trained as a Rebirther at Campbell Hot Springs. My trainer was not Leonard Orr, but two very loving individuals named Barbara Hoff and Robert Varley. The training consisted of repeated rebirthing sessions plus theory sessions with the trainers. I will never forget my first rebirthing session with Barbara. She instructed me on the particular breathing pattern they recommended and I began breathing. About twenty minutes or so into the session, I began to experience exactly what I had experienced in my death experience some eight years before. I felt myself leave my body and travel through space just as I had previously. "So birth and death are really very similar experiences," I thought to myself. After the session, I talked at length with Barbara and we both speculated on the process I had experienced. I felt a special bond with Barbara and was saddened to hear of her recent death by cancer.

After that training, I began rebirthing people and helped to start a one-year seminar on various aspects of rebirthing. Fran and I organized a group of about twenty people who met one weekend a month, each time with a different leader from the national rebirthing community. We covered topics like Creativity, Prosperity, Physical Immortality, Spiritual Psychology and had one week-long training with Leonard Orr. I learned much that helped me work on myself. In August 1978, I attended the first Certification Training for rebirthers at Snowmass, Colorado. Along with fifty other people, I went through a week of accelerated learning. I can remember coming back to my motel room at night and weeping for about an hour. What I saw was people taking responsibility for being totally honest with each other at a feeling level. I now knew that this was what I never experienced in my family of origin. My tears were very healing for me. I began to feel a need to break through some of the barriers to more honest communication with my parents.

Rebirthing My Parents

One night during the training, one of the men spoke about rebirthing his father. He said he had wanted to, but didn't feel ready, and then his dad had a heart attack and almost died. He vowed if his dad recovered that he would take the risk and rebirth him. I reflected on my situation. Six months ago, my parents attended a rebirthing seminar with me, and after the seminar my mother asked if I would rebirth her. I was so shocked that I didn't know what to say but finally answered that I didn't feel that I was ready to do that. I processed my resistance until I realized that if my mother gave up her suffering, I would have to give up my old images and resentments about how she had treated me as a child. In other words, I would have to take total responsibility for any negativity I was still holding onto. I resolved that a big part of the bond I had with my mother was related to the suffering that both of us had done. I had forgotten most of this until I was face to face with the issues that this man raised with the story of his father.

I was moved to action by the man in the training. I wanted to clear up my relationships with my parents while they were still alive. I called them the next morning and proposed that I fly home and rebirth them and anyone else in the family or any of their friends. They agreed, and the following week I was back at home to take the most radical step I had ever taken to heal my relationship with my parents. I had worked on my anger, and my deep sadness had finally surfaced during the Certification Training. I knew it was time to get on with the healing. I didn't know what to expect from this rebirthing experience, but I was open to whatever could happen.

By the end of my eight-day visit, I had rebirthed my mother, my father, my sister, my aunt, my brother-in-law, my nephew and two neighborhood friends of my parents. My mother was first. I was a bit apprehensive as we began, but that soon disappeared as I noticed how quickly she picked up the prescribed breathing pattern. She described her experience in the following way.

"I felt a tingling over my entire body, then I began to feel some twitching and vibrating in my arms and legs. It was a great feeling when I got up and started to walk across the floor. I felt like I was in space, like I was walking on air. I had so much energy that I felt like a different person, so much more alive." During her second session, she processed some fear that grew out of an automobile accident six months before. She said later, "I haven't had any nightmares about the accident since then. Now I can talk about the accident and not shake any more."

My dad was a little less eager than my mother, but he was willing to try it. I was surprised by how quickly he, too, picked up the breathing technique. Following the session he said, "I really felt that I learned to breathe in that first session. I was a mouth-breather since I was a kid because of a nose obstruction. Now I can breathe freely through my nose." During his second session, even more breakthrough occurred. He said, "I had some thoughts about my birth during that session, and I could picture my mother in bed in the room where I was born. I also could picture the iron crib that I slept in as a small boy." In the third session, he experienced a release of old negative thoughts and a dramatic change in his outlook on life. A number of years later, he told me that the rebirthing totally changed his life and helped him become a happier person.

I also rebirthed my sister, who experienced a dramatic shift in her consciousness, as well. She said to me the next evening, "I now know that I am in charge of my life. I never realized that I had so much power and control over what happens to me. It was wonderful."

In addition to all of these changes, I experienced many changes in my own consciousness. I no longer felt any anger toward or need to change my parents in order to suit my needs. I saw what happened to them as taking charge of their lives, and I consciously released them to find their highest good in their own way.

One other completion happened during this visit home. I wrote a series of messages that I always wanted to hear from my parents. Then I asked them to tell me these things while I listened and tape-recorded their words. I knew if I had it on tape I could not deny that I did get what I wanted. Some of the important messages were, "Barry, you do not have to suffer to be happy, healthy and prosperous." This was sort of an ultimate test of my ability to take charge of my life. I was able to ask for what I wanted from my parents in such a way that they were delighted to give it to me.

The most profound changes, however, came in my relationship with them. The rebirthing work created an atmosphere of more open communication and open expression of love, something I had never experienced from them. The following year, I wrote my father a letter on his birthday, expressing all the love and appreciation I could think

182

of. He was moved to tears and called to thank me, saying that he had always wanted to say the things that were in his heart to his father, but he waited and then his father died. I could feel the healing spread to another generation as he shared his sorrow with me.

I also was able to do the same thing with my mother, but it took longer. I had much to work out with myself before I could completely forgive my mother, but finally several years ago, I completed that.

My sister and I also became closer and have continued to share our lives in important ways. We support each other in our efforts to break our family patterns.

The year following all these completions turned out to be one of the most significant of my life. The pace of everything began to pick up. I began the year by publishing two books and I was making media appearances all over the country. I also began to conduct seminars on Breaking Family Patterns and Rebirthing in various cities.

Another Family Pattern Appears

In June, I had planned several seminars in Philadelphia and Washington, D.C., so I asked my parents if I could use their place as home base during that time. I came about a week early just to spend time with them before I went to lead the seminars. The seminar in Philadelphia went as planned, but the one in Washington, D.C. was cancelled when the organizer had a heart attack. This left me with much more time at my parents' home than I had anticipated. In all I had about one month with them. Because I was now free of the distortions I grew up with, I could really see what their relationship was like. One night it hit me. I had a marriage relationship exactly like theirs. I was amazed that I had not seen this pattern before. I was depressed at first, and then began to put it together. I married someone like my mother and I was acting out my father's part. I wanted to change my relationship but couldn't seem to get anywhere. Fran and I talked about this and I found that she really wanted the relationship to stay the same. We had many long discussions in which it became clear that while she was not dissatisfied with our relationship, I certainly was. In the past, I would become confused and unclear about what I wanted when we talked. Now I seemed more clear. I didn't know what to do with this clarity, so I waited. I didn't have to wait long, but I never thought the information I was looking for would come to me from an eight-hundred-year-old man.

Gathering Allies

As participants in the year-long rebirthing seminar, Steven and Trina Kamp came to Colorado Springs to present a seminar. The only unusual thing about this was that Trina was a medium and had various entities speak through her. I had not met them before, but one day Steven called me and suggested that I attend a trance circle in Denver several weeks in advance of the Colorado Springs seminar so that I could better advertise their seminar.

Dr. Duran and Divorce

I arrived at the house where the seminar was held, and at about dusk the trance circle began. After a group song, Trina dropped into a trance and this man's voice started to "come through" her. His name was Dr. Duran and he was a physician who supposedly lived in London in the twelfth century. He began going around the room greeting everyone, and when he came to me, he greeted me and proceeded to tell me that we were old friends from past lifetimes and, over the course of the evening, repeated many things about me that he could not have known. I was shocked. Later that evening, he said to me, "Barry, I also want to tell you that you are about to have the relationship that you have always wanted."

Crossing the Threshold

As I drove home, I pondered all the messages that Dr. Duran had given me. Fran was waiting eagerly for me when I got home. I began to share with her what Duran had told me about my long-dreamed relationship, which led us into a four and one-half hour discussion. By the end of that time, we came to a mutual decision to get a divorce. We both realized very clearly that night that we each wanted a different relationship and that neither of us was wrong or bad for wanting something different than the other. The decision to separate seemed complete and clean. For me this decision was crossing the threshold, venturing into the unknown. I had an internal feeling of rightness for this decision, but at the same time I was aware of the risks involved.

The next two months were filled with new challenges as I moved out of the house and entered the single world for the first time in over twenty years. I was really scared, but I decided to take everything one step at a time and live for the moment.

My Marriage to Barbara

I dated a number of women, including my old friend, Barbara, who was now single. She had separated and divorced several years earlier and had given up on me ever leaving my marriage. It didn't take either of us long to realize that the old feelings we once had for each other were still strong. We both were dating other people but found ourselves wanting to be with each other more and more. After several months, we stopped dating others and began to spend all our free time together. About six months later, we eloped to Reno and began our married life together. I truly believed that I had found my soul mate and finally had the relationship I had always wanted, just the way Dr. Duran had predicted.

The Road of Trials

Unfortunately, the dream I had was shattered rather quickly. We started life together with five teenagers living with us (three of Barbara's and two of mine). The stress of work, parenting and adjusting to married life added up to a very busy life that started to take its toll on both of us. Barbara became hypercritical of me. Our sexual relationship became difficult. What happened was that our relationship had gotten close enough for a new wave of family patterns to surface. Barbara remembered being an incest victim as a child and often would have flashbacks during our lovemaking. She was usually unable to continue with lovemaking when this would happen, leaving me feeling angry and frustrated. She was not letting me fulfill my dream, and so I had very little patience with her problem. I wanted her to fix the problem and suggested therapy. During this time we did couples therapy, family therapy and individual therapy.

Family Patterns Surface with Barbara

Finally, through my own individual therapy, I began to see what was going on. I had regressed in the relationship by becoming a butler, taking care of Barbara and not taking care of my own needs and wants. This co-dependency remained as my more persistent family pattern. As a parentized child, I was devoted to taking care of others and denying my own needs. I really was ready to break this one, once and for all.

I remained attendant to her needs, but I began to ask her for nurturing and support as well as being more straight with her about

185

my own feelings. I had tremendous love and respect for Barbara. She worked about as hard as anyone I had known to deal with her family patterns. She was very remorseful about the brokenness she brought into the relationship. At times she told me she feared that she would never conquer the fears that so ruled her life and interfered with our intimacy.

One night I experienced a tremendous breakthrough with Barbara. I stopped resisting her problem and fully surrendered to her. I received her fully without resistance. I felt a tremendous overflow of love and she was able to respond with equal love. I had never understood what surrender really meant. However, this breakthrough brought results that I certainly was not ready to deal with. Barbara was unable to sustain her closeness and she began to get more and more despondent. Several times she told me she did not want to go on living, and I would usually try to talk her out of her depression or suggest some new way to work on the problem that we hadn't tried before.

The Dark Night of the Soul

It was the day before Easter in 1983 and we had plans to go skiing and stay overnight at a ski resort. That morning as we packed to leave, Barbara seemed distant and even suggested that we not go. I was eager to go, so she agreed. On the drive up we talked about many things, including mutual projects on which we were working. As we rode up the ski lift, Barbara asked me to help her edit the book on which she was working. Early in the afternoon, we were skiing down an intermediate level slope when it happened. I was ahead of her and I hit a patch of sheer ice and went tumbling down the hill. When I stopped sliding, I looked for Barbara and saw her lying in a heap about thirty feet to my right. When I got to her she was unconscious and I saw that she was bleeding through her ski pants. For the next twenty hours, she hung on to life as I stayed by her side in the hospital. Finally at about eleven o'clock on Easter morning, she died.

The bottom had just fallen out of my life. For months after her death, I too wanted to die. I could not find much reason to live except to help take care of the grief of our children and friends. I went over the accident a million times in my mind during those months, and some new awareness began to emerge. There was no reason for the accident. There were no witnesses, but the details seemed impossible.

She had a huge laceration of the femoral artery to her right leg, but there was no puncture of her ski pants and no one could account for how the laceration occurred. I began to piece together what Barbara had told me during the week prior to the accident. From this I concluded that Barbara knew she was going to die and had tried to tell me. She was despairing during that time, and each time I tried to get her to think of more positive solutions. Even the morning of the ski trip, she tried to talk me out of going. During the twenty hours in the hospital, although she was not conscious and I could not talk to her until a brief time near the end, she would drift back and forth between life and death. Her heart stopped in the ambulance and she was revived with CPR. At times, she would seem to get stronger, only to slip away again.

I was angry at God for taking her away and at times I would rage at God. I was also angry at Barbara for leaving me. I was angry at her family of origin for the condemnation of her and refusing to deal with the incest issue. I was angry at everyone, including myself, for not listening to Barbara's death wish. Then I asked myself, "Did I really want to die?" The answer was "No." I realized that it wasn't my time and that for some reason unknown to me, I wanted to live.

The Sacred Marriage

The next twelve months were a time of tremendous healing and growth for me. I realized that one of the strongest dynamics in my relationship with Barbara was co-dependency. I realized that I had projected my ideal feminine image on her and she had done her best to match my projected image. Conversely, Barbara had projected her ideal masculine image on me and I had done my best to fulfill it. When Barbara died, I felt that my feminine side died with her. I felt like half a person and tried to find someone else on whom I could project my feminine side, but I couldn't find anyone who measured up.

Finally, I decided to take back what I had projected and learn to integrate it. This meant I had to learn to nurture myself and begin to enjoy my own feminine-side company. For a while, I didn't even want nurturing and comfort from a woman. I experienced their attempts as smothering and efforts to take away my pain. By contrast, I found that nurturing from men did not have this quality. I learned that men would empathize with me, but rarely would sympathize with me.

They would "feel" my pain with me and were not interested in making it go away. I realized that I no longer needed or wanted the mothering kind of nurturing that many women had to offer. I realized that I had settled for this kind of relationship and now I knew that I wanted a different relationship with a woman.

Taking Back the True Self

It was during this time that I did my final completion work with my mother. I realized that I had not completely let go of my attachment to old relationship patterns with her. What I had to do was take back my True Self and not wait for a woman (my mother) to take care of me. Despite all the growth I had accomplished, I still settled for a co-dependent relationship with Barbara. Some further therapy helped me to see this clearly, and so I began to think about what kind of a relationship I did want. I also realized that I was developing a new relationship with myself and that this process had to come first. That involved forgiving myself for the mistakes I had made previously and forgiving others, including Barbara, for deserting me. During the next four months, I learned to develop a solid relationship with myself.

However, I realized I needed to feel complete with Barbara by having an opportunity to talk to her. I wasn't even able to say good-bye to her when she died, and this lack of completion seemed to haunt me. Finally the opportunity came. A friend of mine suggested that I ask my spirit guides to arrange a meeting with Barbara. I thought about this and decided it was worth a try. I had practiced bringing Barbara back through my sensory memory of her. I could remember how she looked, sounded, felt, smelled and tasted. When I used all my senses, I could feel her presence very strongly. So I focused all my senses on bringing her back and then asked my spirit guides to take me to her. I experienced being led by one of my guides into a rather dark and damp cave. Finally, we came out into a large room filled with mist.

I waited and eventually heard Barbara's voice coming from the mist. I could not see her and asked her to come out where I could see her. She said, "No, not now, for you may be frightened by my changed appearance." She said,

> I knew I was going to die. I knew it for about a year, but I didn't want to accept it. I tried not to think about it and when it was no longer possible for me to block out the thoughts, I tried to talk to

188

you about it. You weren't able to listen to my fears. I am sorry I
had to leave you, but I had no choice. I could not stand the pain
in my body any longer, and I realized I had to leave my body
behind me before I could go any further. Please forgive me for
leaving so suddenly with all the unfinished business I left for you
to clean up. I wish it could have been done some other way. I was
still ambivalent even after the ski accident. I didn't want to live
as an invalid after the accident. I will always love you.

I was filled with tremendous sadness and joy. I could hardly speak,
but finally I said, "Barbara, I am so relieved to be able to talk to you
and feel complete. I may need to talk to you some more before I'm
finished with this. Please forgive me for not wanting to hear your
fears. I was too scared of losing you to be of much help. I do love you
and release you to go on with your life on the other side. Some day
we may be joined again."

Then Barbara laughed in her characteristic way and said to me,
"It gives me great pleasure to tell you that you will not have to be
alone for very long. They are trying to find someone to send to you.
Also, she will have evolved to a higher consciousness and will not
have the same problems that I had." I was shocked and thrilled by
what she was saying. I asked, "Who are THEY?" She replied,
"THEY are the members of our soul group." Then I asked, "How will
I find this person?" She responded by saying, "You will not have to
look for her. She will find you and you will recognize her by her vibration, which will be much like mine." Finally I asked, "How long
will I have to wait until she shows up?" She said, "It is not possible to
say exactly, but it shouldn't be very long." We said our tearful goodbyes and I felt a sense of completion to the first phase of healing.

Fall Into Grace

During the next several months, I experienced a tremendous growth
spurt. I attended a week-long training with Dr. Jean Houston in Chicago and experienced even more completion with Barbara. During the
training, Jean conducted a healing session for those who were grieving
the loss of a loved one. We were asked to imagine a bridge with our-
self at one end and the loved one at the other. I began walking in my
imagination toward Barbara, knowing that I would meet her in the
middle of the bridge. I could see Barbara in her wedding dress, with
long, white hair hanging to her waist. Jean instructed us to exchange

189

vows that remarried us for eternal life. Then we said our goodbyes and each turned and walked back to the separate ends of the bridge, knowing that the bonds between us were not broken. I remember feeling like some burden had lifted from me and, as the others came back into the seminar room, I got up and danced freely to the music from "Flashdance," and then the song "Memory" was played. I fell into the arms of a woman who had just lost her husband and we sobbed together through the whole song.

The Return of Consciousness

After returning from Chicago, I had signed up for Jean Houston's "Mystery School" training in New York. This meant flying to New York one weekend a month during 1984 to meet with 140 other people. The Mystery School was a tremendous help for my healing as I began developing a nationwide network of fellow journeyers on the path of transformation. It was a time of transformation as I let go of my old attachments and developed new tools and new friends.

That summer, I went to Europe for the first time and traveled to many places that I wanted to see. I fell in love with Switzerland, and I began to dream about coming back to Switzerland during my sabbatical leave from the University, which was still a year away. I came back from Europe feeling ready to get on with my life. I began dreaming about what kind of life I really wanted. I constructed about five or six scenarios of my future, and at the time, I remember thinking that any of the ones I constructed would be exciting. I felt free to really decide my own future.

Developing New Patterns

I decided that I would watch for things that happened to me that seemed to pull me toward any of the scenarios. I didn't have long to wait before I got a strong pull. I flew back to New York in early September for the monthly Mystery School session. On Friday evening, we were doing free movement to music when I spun around and my arm hit a woman in the chest who was also spinning near me. I apologized briefly and moved on, but the next morning when I saw her again, I approached her to talk some more. We laughed about the bumping incident and chatted briefly about the seminar. Her name was Jean Wilson and I remembered meeting her briefly at the June session, but she seemed so much different now. I wasn't sure why, but

I began to feel drawn to her. Several times, I found myself standing near Jean or talking with a mutual friend when Jean came by. As the weekend continued, I felt a familiar energy vibration whenever I was near her. We didn't speak to one another again until Sunday afternoon when the weekend session was ending.

I wanted to tell her about my feelings but was scared. As I saw her getting ready to leave, I decided to act. I walked up to Jean and gave her a hug and a kiss. She seemed a bit startled but I continued, saying that I was attracted to her and wanted to get to know her better. Then I said, "There doesn't seem to be much opportunity to get to know each other in this setting. Is there any chance you might come to Colorado soon?" She answered, "Not really, but you never know about these things."

On the airplane back to Colorado, I began to think about how forward I had been and felt afraid that perhaps I had been too forward. I decided to open my heart to Jean by writing her a long letter explaining my uncharacteristic forwardness and my recent decision to be a risk-taker and act more on my feelings. I explained that Barbara's death meant I had loved and lost, so that fear of rejection no longer held me back. After mailing the letter, I again questioned myself, realizing how vulnerable I was feeling. Was I setting myself up for another rejection? Could I really handle another rejection? Well, Jean must have sensed my vulnerability because she wrote back immediately, saying an opportunity to come to Colorado the next month had suddenly appeared. We began to write and talk on the phone in preparation for her visit.

In the meantime, we had another Mystery School weekend, and we agreed to meet at the airport in New York and make the two-hour drive up to the conference site together in a carpool of participants. As I drove the car with Jean beside me in the front, the other three people in the back seemed far away. I felt this intense energy between us the whole way to the seminar. It was familiar and yet different. As it turned out, some parts of the weekend activities were cancelled, leaving us with hours together to talk and get to know each other. As we talked, I was "blown away." Jean had many of the same kinds of dreams about the future that I had. On every level, there seemed to be harmony and connection. We left that weekend together as friends, both eagerly awaiting our extended time together in Colorado.

Marriage to Jean

We had planned ten days together in Colorado, but by the time four days had passed, we knew we were going to get married. I had never experienced such a complete knowing of another person so quickly. We made our plans to get married on Thanksgiving Day and also asked Jean Houston to perform a spiritual wedding for us when our training group traveled to Egypt and Greece in January.

The Shared Journey

This was another time of intense growth and change for me. For the next several months, Jean and I were never apart, as we built an intense bonding and love between us. I recognized this as the kind of relationship that I had always wanted and finally I had it. My life was enriched beyond belief and our love and relationship just kept on growing and deepening. At the same time, I was still dealing with the grief of Barbara's death and, fortunately, Jean was comfortable with me talking freely about my feelings of loss and grief.

I took a six month's sabbatical leave from the University in January of 1986 to go with Jean to Switzerland to study with Dr. Arnold Mindell, who had developed a meta-theory that blends well with the Transpersonal Relationship Therapy that I had developed. We continued to work on our relationship and to heal old wounds. During that time, we both worked intensely on our death patterns with Dr. Mindell, who specializes in work with dying people. We learned much more about another layer of death patterning we learned from our family of origin. Jean went through a breakdown/breakthrough experience while we were there. It was so profound an experience for her that she decided that Jean had died and she changed her name to Janae to symbolize the rebirth of her new consciousness.

We continue to work cooperatively to bring to the surface deeper levels of patterning and to bring them into our conscious awareness. We both see this as an exciting part of our relationship and truly a lifelong process. This is a journey that really has no end, only more and more awareness and appreciation for the complexity of life and the depth of the human psyche. We know we will have many more adventures together and separately as we grow up and become more conscious of who we really are.

Armstrong, Louise. 1983. *The Home Front.* New York: McGraw–Hill Book Company.

Ballentine, Rudolph. 1978. *Diet and Nutrition: A Holistic Approach.* Honesdale, PA: The Himalayan Institute.

Bradshaw, John. 1988. *The Family.* Dearfield Beach, FL: Health Commission, Inc.

Brothers, Joyce. 1984. "Why Men Abuse Women." *Parade Magazine,* November 11, pp 4–9.

Campbell, Joseph. 1968. *Hero With A Thousand Faces.* Princeton, NJ: Princeton University Press.

Evans-Wentz, W. Y. 1960. *Tibetan Book of the Dead.* New York: Oxford University Press.

Forward, Susan and Buck, Craig. 1978. *Betrayal of Innocence.* New York: Penguin Books.

Goldstein, Joseph. 1976. *Reexperience of Insight: A Natural Unfolding.* Santa Cruz, CA: Unity Press.

Grof, Stanislav. 1976. *Realms of the Human Unconscious.* New York: E. P. Dutton & Co., Inc.

Gruenwald, H. 1977. "On the Character Fault of Willfulness in Children." In *Black Pedagogy,* Rutschley, Katherine. Berlin.

Hay, Louise. 1984. *You Can Heal Your Life.* Farmingdale, N.Y.: Coleman Publishing.

Hendricks, Gay and Weinhold, Barry. 1982. *Transpersonal Approaches to Counseling and Psychotherapy.* Denver: Love Publishing Company.

Hillman, James. 1979. The Feeling Function. In *Jung's Typology,* M. L. Von Frantz and J. Hillman. Irving, TX: Spring Publications, Inc.

Hillman, James. 1975. *Loose Ends: Primary Papers in Archetypal Psychology.* New York/Zurich: Spring Publications, Inc.

Hills, Christopher. 1980. *Creative Conflict.* Boulder Creek, CA: University of the Trees Press.

Hoffman, Bob. 1976. *Getting Divorced From Mother and Dad.* New York: E. P. Dutton & Co., Inc.

Kaplan, Louise. 1978. *Oneness and Separateness: From Infant to Individual.* New York: Simon and Schuster.

Kelly, John. 1979. "Baby '79: What Every Woman (and man) Should Know About Childbirth." *Ladies Home Journal,* January, pp 105–107.

Klaus, Marshall and Kennell, John. 1976. *Material-infant Bonding*. St. Louis: The C. V. Mosby Company.

Lad, Vasant. 1984. *Ayurveda: The Science of Self-healing*. Santa Fe, NM: Lotus Press.

Laing, R.D. 1965. "Mystification, Confusion and Conflict." In *Intensive Family Therapy: Theoretical and Practical Aspects,* edited by I. Bosyoomenyi-Nagy and J. Framo New York: Harper and Row.

Lidz, Theodore. 1968. *The Person*. New York: Basic Books, Inc.

Madsen, Clifford and Madsen, Charles. 1975. *Parents and Children, Love and Discipline*. Northbrook, IL: AHM Publishing Corporation.

Mahler, Margaret. 1968. *On Human Symbiosis and the Vicissitudes of Individuation*. New York: International University Press.

Masterson, James. 1981. *The Narcissistic and Borderline Disorders*. New York: Brunner/Mazel, Publishers.

Miller, Alice. 1981. *Prisoners of Childhood*. New York: Basic Books, Inc.

Miller, Alice. 1983. *For Your Own Good*. New York: Farrar, Straus, Giroux.

Mindell, Arnold. 1985. *Process Oriented Meditation*. Unpublished manuscript. pp 71–73.

Nietzsche, Fredrich. 1955. *The Birth of Tragedy and the Genealogy of Morals*. Translated by Francis Golffing. New York: Doubleday, Garden City.

Pearce, Joseph Chilton. 1977. *Magical Child*. New York: E. P. Dutton and Co., Inc.

Purpura, Dominick. 1975. "Consciousness." *Behavior Today,* June 2, p 494.

Ray, Sondra. 1980. *Loving Relationships*. Millbrae, CA: Celestial Arts.

Salem, Maria Z. and Adams, Raymond D. 1966. "New Horizons in the Neurology of Childhood." *Perspectives in Biology and Medicine,* Spring, pp 384–410.

Sheehy, Gail. 1976. *Passages*. New York: E. P. Dutton & Co., Inc.

Sontag, Lester. 1963. "Somatophysics of Personality and Body Function." *Vita Humana,* 4 (2), 1–10.

Stierlin, H. 1976. "The Dynamics of Owning and Disowning Psychoanalytic and Family Perspectives." *Family Process,* 15, pp 277–288.

Stott, Dennis. 1973. "Follow-up Study From Barth of the Effects of

Prenatal Stresses." *Developmental Medicine and Child Neurology*, 15, pp 770–787.

Strau, Murray, et al. 1980. *Behind Closed Doors: Violence in the American Family*. New York: Anchor Press/Doubleday.

Sulzer, J. 1977. "An Essay on the Education and Instruction of Children." In *Black Pedagogy*. Rutschley, Katharine. Berlin.

Verny, Thomas. 1984. *The Secret Life of the Unborn Child*. New York: Delta Books.

Walker, Lenore E. 1979. *The Battered Woman*. New York: Harper Colophon Books.

Weinhold, Barry and Andresen, Gail. 1979. *Threads*. New York: Richard Marck Publishers.

Weinhold, Barry & Elliott, Lynn. 1979. *Transpersonal Communication*. Englewood Cliffs, NJ: Prentice-Hall.

Weinhold, Barry. 1982. *A Transpersonal Approach to Counselor Education*. Colorado Springs, CO: (Self published).

Weinhold, Barry and Beggs, James (eds.) 1984. *Transforming Persons and Programs*. Alexandria, VA: The AACD Press.

Zaleski, Philip. 1984. "A New Age Interview: Elizabeth Kübler-Ross." *New Age Journal*, November, pp 39–44.